C000227853

From Hole
to Whole

Embracing the Transformational
Power of Grief and Loss

Joy Sackett Wood

R^ethink

First published in Great Britain in 2020 by Rethink Press
(www.rethinkpress.com)

© Copyright Joy Sackett Wood

All rights reserved. No part of this publication may be
reproduced, stored in or introduced into a retrieval system,
or transmitted, in any form, or by any means (electronic,
mechanical, photocopying, recording or otherwise) without
the prior written permission of the publisher.

The right of Joy Sackett Wood to be identified as the author
of this work has been asserted by her in accordance with the
Copyright, Designs and Patents Act 1988.

This book is sold subject to the condition that it shall not,
by way of trade or otherwise, be lent, resold, hired out, or
otherwise circulated without the publisher's prior consent
in any form of binding or cover other than that in which it
is published and without a similar condition including this
condition being imposed on the subsequent purchaser.

Illustrations courtesy of Sarah Royle

Explosion icon in Grief Curve Diagrams by Aisyah from the
Noun Project

This book is dedicated to Josh.
May you come to feel
the transformational power of love and healing
intended here for you

Contents

Foreword

The book you are holding in your hands opens a doorway to a whole new way of dealing with grief after the death of a loved one. *From Hole To Whole* offers a cutting-edge approach to understanding firstly how, like a phoenix rising from the ashes, we can grow from our grieving process. Secondly, how we can safeguard our business during that time of disruption and finally, how we can continue to have an enriched, meaningful and growing relationship with our deceased loved one.

Joy and I became friends more than thirty-five years ago when our daughters attended primary school together. Over the following years we became a huge source of mutual support for one another. I had just managed to extricate myself from a very acrimonious marriage and divorce and Joy was in the process of doing the same. In spite of the numerous challenges, we both went back into higher education, obtaining degrees and professional qualifications, and forged new lives for ourselves.

We both shared an ongoing interest in people, humanity and spirituality, continuing to the present day. Joy found herself a new career as a teacher of cultural studies, which she held for many years before further study to become a counsellor and hypnotherapist and subsequently building her own very successful private practice with her husband John at Swans Therapy in Bournemouth.

I shall never forget the day when Joy arrived on my doorstep in Plymouth, in a state of profound sorrow and shock, telling me that her beautiful son Jack had died. She stayed with me for the following few weeks while she meticulously and lovingly took care of every detail of Jack's funeral. It was truly heart rending yet breathtaking to watch the outpouring of her grief into a tenderly composed and very personal expression of her love for Jack, in a painting she did on his coffin and the most warm and heartfelt funeral I have ever attended (and being Irish, I have attended many).

I am so delighted that Joy has further transmuted her grief in sharing her deep learning with you, the reader, in this book. I have watched her journey over the time since Jack's death and am full of admiration for how she has taken the base metal of her sorrow and distilled it into the gold you now hold in your hands.

Using an acronym of the word 'RESILIENCE' to progress through the layers of the book is truly inspired as it is this amazing human characteristic that gets us through many traumas in our lives. Joy clearly demonstrates that our own resilience can be nurtured and grown to make us strong enough to not only survive, but to bounce back from even our darkest times. The idea of building layers of resilience to fill the 'hole' left by the grief is a wonderful concept and using the different coloured layers as the book progresses demonstrates this very clearly.

As a counsellor with many years of experience myself, I fully appreciate the difficulty of working with bereaved clients, each with their own memories, fears and ideas about how the world expects them to grieve. The truth is that there is no right or wrong way to get through this most difficult of times, but there are more, or less, helpful ways. The death of a loved one is a process that we will all need to go through at some time in our lives and a very personal journey that everyone will deal with in their own way.

This book does not try to tell the reader what to do, but gently guides and offers suggestions and advice on the process of grief as clearly explained in the changing format of the progressive 'grief curve' diagrams, but that is only part of the story. The revelations later in the book, along with convincing evidence that death is not the end of life, truly make this book a 'must read' and then read again.

Joy's spirituality shines through as she explains the new relationship with her deceased son. How they have learned to communicate in a different way which has become a source of love, help, and learning in the continuing cycle of life and death.

When someone close to you dies, your life will never be the same again, but it will go on. If you are prepared to open your heart and your mind to new possibilities, you may find that it can be so much more than you ever dreamed of.

Grace Chatting, BA (Hons) CQSW MBACP Snr. Accred, founder of Western Women Mean Business

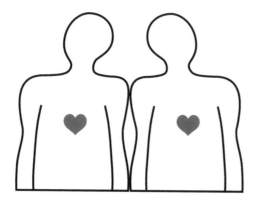

Introduction

When someone close to you dies, whether due to a long-term illness (and you thought you were prepared for their passing), or a sudden and unexpected event, the impact is naturally unsettling and distressing. The anguish of finding yourself without the person and the love you shared can be excruciating. You may wonder how you are going to cope.

This is the central question this book will address for you.

Most of us have suffered loss of some kind or another, but the loss of a key figure in our lives is particularly hard to come to terms with. Moreover, if we have additional responsibilities such as running our own business or holding down a job as well as taking care of our family, it can be much harder. Women, being the main carers within society, can find it more difficult than men and often lose themselves in the process of grief, which inevitably prolongs the pain and suffering.

At the time of writing, we are in the midst of the COVID-19 pandemic. What this has highlighted is how disruption to daily routines, work and education impacts on relationships and people's mental and physical wellbeing. The negative effects of lockdown created a great deal of fear and anxiety due to isolation and lack of human contact, especially for those living on their own, which in itself can be a source of grief and loss, as well as raising tensions causing aggressive and violent responses in others.

Fears of and actual financial and business loss, redundancies, lack of employment, fear of and loss of homes, opportunities and education have all caused a surge of grief reactions and experiences, not to mention the fear of and actual loss of a loved one to COVID-19. A rupture in any relationship or situation causes feelings of grief, fear, sadness, separation, isolation and loneliness.

This book was initiated by the sudden and unexpected death of my son Jack a day before his fortieth birthday, on 27 October 2018. You may wonder how I can even write such a book, that it must simply be a vehicle to purge my pain, but I say no! Through my personal experience, I've learnt how to build a multi-dimensional layer of inner resilience.

I was inspired to use RESILIENCE as a model for this book while reflecting on Jack and attending to my own grief. Sitting in my special place of peace and solace, the beautiful cabin my husband John lovingly built, aptly named 'Peace Haven', I began reading a book by George Bonanno called *The Other Side of Sadness*.[1] In his book, Bonanno writes about a woman whose daughter had died in the Twin Towers attacks. He interviewed her as part of his intensive research on grief and grieving, curious about how quickly she had returned to her daily activities and commitments while others had remained highly traumatised by their grief experiences in losing their loved ones in such a horrific way. She said she was very **resilient** and explained that she had been through a lot of adversities and had learnt to bounce back quickly from life's 'knocks'. Besides, her daughter wouldn't have wanted her mother to lose her job and would understand she had others dependant on her and needed to get on with her life. Bonanno was so impressed by this that he concluded that the length of the time of grief recovery depended solely on a person's individual **resilience**: their ability

1   GA Bonanno, *The Other Side of Sadness: What the new science of bereavement tells us about life after loss* (Basic Books, 2010)

to overcome shock and trauma and come to terms with the disruption in their lives.

This made absolute sense to me as I could relate to it personally, having overcome much adversity and trauma in my own life. As I pondered on this, I remembered Jack once saying to me that he admired me for my inner strength, that I was the 'strongest person he has ever known'.

Resilience is what I want to pass on to you. Not just from what I already knew through my professional therapeutic training and experience, but also what I gained through my deeper journey into self-development and self-discovery – a journey that has taken me beyond any of my previous experiences or dreams.

My personal grief journey has led me to amazing spiritual depths and levels of consciousness I had never explored before. This book is about those experiences and the exciting discoveries I have made. It is about how this journey changed my life for ever for the better. Essentially, it is about building resilience to overcome the trauma of grief, successfully evolving and transforming ourselves through the process. It is a self-help book for those who have experienced the death of a loved one and are looking for guidance, help and support.

If you are running your own business, an employer, a manager, an employee, a colleague in corporate or small business, a friend, a therapist working in the field of bereavement, or just interested in learning more about grief and personal, emotional, rational and spiritual growth, this book is for you. Through its pages, you will learn and understand so much more about grief and grieving, and what a wonderfully multi-dimensional person you are.

When Jack died, it was the worst thing I could imagine happening in my life. I have an adult daughter, Jeneen, and a husband, John, a private therapy practice established in 2008, and an extended family with needs as well as my own to consider. It is true to say that being a professionally trained psychotherapist, counsellor and complementary therapist myself who has worked successfully with many clients experiencing grief helped me, but this did not diminish my raw and very real pain in the initial stages following his death. There is no competition with pain. Pain is pain and grief is grief; there is no escaping it. It felt like a big **hole** had been carved out of my chest and stomach; the pain was physical. Fortunately, I was aware that there is, in counselling terms, a 'grief process', so I decided to surrender myself absolutely and go with the flow of that process.

In doing this, I learnt so much more about grief, which I want to share with you in this book. I discovered how to grieve healthily and successfully, and how to keep my business and life functioning. I learnt how to build even greater resilience than I believed I had before this life-changing grief event, and how to develop and strengthen this resilience.

Resilience is such a positive aspect of grief, enabling us to rise above the pain, reduce emotional suffering and evolve through the transition to gain a higher consciousness, empowerment and spiritual growth. In other words, we positively evolve as a human being as part of our soul journey, and so become **whole**.

Building resilience begins by being aware of how the brain works; how the trauma of grief affects our brain and nervous system, which then impact on our emotions and affect the physiology of our body to cause our spirit to retract. This disturbing assault on our inner being can be reversed.

There are many books on grief and grieving. How is this book different? I will take you beyond the accepted therapeutically known grief process, showing you how to evolve as a person, undergo a personal transformation and develop your soul through your grief. This book is all about you becoming aware that you are a multi-dimensional being – a person who functions on many levels – and a vibrational-energy being who, following deep sadness and sorrow, is able to live a life filled with love, happiness and immense joy. You can have an ongoing relationship with your loved one, albeit a different one, as I did through my own personal journey. I will offer suggestions, tools, techniques, case studies, scientific evidence, personal insights and knowledge to enlighten you.

Throughout this book, I will take you through my journey of experiencing a different relationship with my son which has been both remarkable and unexpected. This represents a personal story in which my son made it clear to me that he didn't want me to grieve, but wanted me to learn and understand. Alongside this, I will share the ten levels of my RESILIENCE model, which will support you through each stage of grief to spiritual enlightenment.

Each of the ten levels of RESILIENCE is represented in a chapter:

♥ Response – understanding various responses, coping with shock and trauma, attending to important practical matters.

♥ Education – learning how grief trauma affects your mind, body and emotions.

♥ Surrender – accepting the situation. Making choices, developing the courage and determination to grieve your way in a healthy way.

♥ Initiate – strategies to help you cope, using initiative and understanding, and supporting self, family, friends, colleagues, staff, employees, etc.

♥ Love – self-love, self-nurturing, taking care of yourself. This is all about making healthy choices for your own wellbeing so you are able to love and care for others and your business/work life.

♥ Intuition – finding meaning and questioning through faith, religion, spiritual beliefs (spiritual meaning shifts in perception) and science.

♥ Empowerment – confidence, strength, new learnings, knowledge, expansion (personal growth).

♥ Next level – greater understanding of personal development and experiences as a conscious being (mindset growth).

♥ Change – this covers transition, spiritual interconnections, advancement, new paradigms, a different relationship with your loved one (spiritual growth).

♥ Evolution – evidence of the continuing soul journey and a release from **hole** (feeling hollow) to feeling **whole** on each level. Conscious awareness of being a multi-dimensional vibrational-energy being (energy growth).

Now you know what to expect from this book, let's make a start.

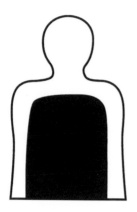

ONE

Building The First Layer
Of RESILIENCE

Response – understanding various responses, coping with shock and trauma, attending to important practical matters.

Resilience means inner strength or resolve, a developed capacity to endure emotional challenges. It is all about helping yourself to understand your emotional responses – what is happening to you. This way you will be better prepared to help yourself as and when you need to.

There is a process of grief with different stages that may be a helpful guide for you, but grief is a deeply personal experience. The loss of a loved one brings about a kaleidoscopic range of emotions and grief is not linear; you will experience an emotional swing from one stage to another and back again, sometimes within the same day.

In the first layer of RESILIENCE, **response**, I will help you through the initial stage of grief: shock, trauma and denial. In addition, I will introduce you to understanding how your brain responds to the impact of trauma and discuss how this influences your decision making and may impact on your wellbeing, offering some suggestions to help you support and protect yourself, your family and your work life during this most vulnerable stage of your grief.

The Grief Curve and your emotions

When your loved one dies, understanding your emotional responses to what needs to be done practically is important. The decisions that you make at this time could have a long-term impact on you and your life, family, friends and any other loved ones, and your work. By tuning in and developing your self-awareness, you will become much more confident and feel more able to handle this particularly difficult time.

In her 1969 book *On Death and Dying*,[2] Elisabeth Kübler-Ross identified the five different stages of grief. In essence, she suggested that grief emotions are similar for each of us:

- **Denial**: shock, disbelief that the death of a loved one has occurred

- **Anger** that someone we love is no longer with us

- **Bargaining**: all the what ifs and regrets

- **Depression**: sadness from the loss

- **Acceptance**: acknowledging the reality of the loss

Kübler-Ross described this process in the form of a Grief Curve, descending through the emotions into depression before moving back upwards to normal life. Although simplistic, this model remains a good way to explain the process of grief to people, and that understanding can bring them some comfort in a most difficult time.

---

2   E Kübler-Ross, *On Death and Dying* (Macmillan, 1969)

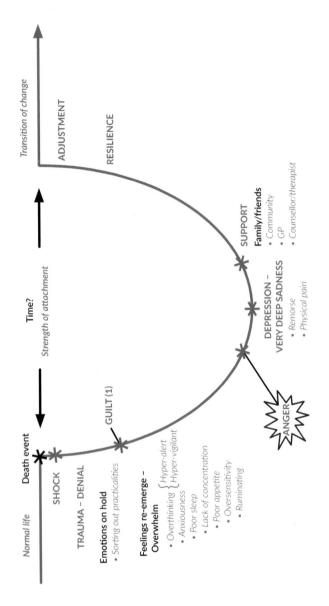

Grief Curve, Diagram 1A

Due to my professional experiences in working thera-peutically with grieving clients, I have found it helpful to include additional stages and aspects to Kübler-Ross's five, which you can see on Grief Curve, Diagram 1A. I will expand on this model as we progress through the book.

As you can see from the diagram, the length of the grief process has no time span as it depends entirely on the bond of the relationship. There are different kinds of death responses depending on who has died. When a partner dies, it is different to when a parent or grandparent dies, which is different to when other members of the family such as a sibling or a cousin dies. The most traumatic experiences tend to be when the death is unexpected, especially when it's out of the natural order like a young child dying. As parents, we certainly don't expect our child to die before us.

By its nature, love is the most powerful of emotions, so understanding the grief process and how it works helps when you lose a loved one. When I counsel clients, I begin by giving them an explanation of the Grief Curve as most people feel confused and challenged by their strong and diverse emotions. I often hear them say that it feels like they are losing control of their minds.

You may be able to relate to this, so let's refer to the Grief Curve as a tool to help you understand which stage of your grief journey you are presently or have previously been in. This will help you to make sense of your experiences in the near- or long-term future.

PERSONAL EXPERIENCE

When I received the news of my son Jack's death, I had just arrived home from the airport following a beautiful two-week holiday in Gran Canaria with my husband John. In the second week we were joined by my grandson, his partner and their three-year-old daughter. It was 4pm and we had literally just put our suitcases down in our living room when the call came through from my ex-husband, informing us about my son's death.

John took the call, and I knew instantly from the tone of his voice and his choice of words what the news was about. For my ex-husband to call him had to mean bad news.

The guttural noise that came out of my mouth was totally unrecognisable to me. I have never experienced or heard anything like it in my life. I remember so vividly reacting instantaneously and violently, screaming and screaming out loud, unashamedly, oblivious to who may have overheard me. Shaking my head in disbelief, saying, 'No, no, no, please no'. This was the most terrible information I could ever hear. It had to be wrong, wrong, wrong. Please no, not this. This cannot be real; this isn't happening to me.

Looking pleadingly at my husband, I begged with my eyes for him to tell me something different. Let this not be true – not now, not ever. The expression reflected back at me in my husband's eyes said it all. No words could he find to console me, except, 'Sorry, I am so, so sorry'.

I don't know how long this went on for, but as I write, my body is remembering the pain. It's hot and raw. I can feel pressure in my chest and tears erupt in my eyes. The body remembers. This is indeed the worst moment of my life that I am recalling. In a split second, it felt like someone had ripped my heart out and gutted me.

This was trauma. As a person who is usually appropriately in control of my emotions, I really was overwhelmed. My mind just couldn't comprehend it. Only hours before on the aeroplane, I had been pondering and planning how I was going to celebrate Jack's fortieth birthday with him in Devon the very next day. This was all so wrong, so horrible, so impossible, so traumatic. I had to let the initial shock subside before I could even talk to his sister about it.

The brain's immediate thought response to trauma

From a neurological point of view, my brain had been flooded with cortisol, a chemical which enables an extra surge of energy to boost the function of our muscles and adrenalin and get us into fight or flight mode. But as there was no way of fighting or running from this danger and threat, the information overwhelmed me with emotion, which is a perfectly normal response to over stimulation. This is exactly how we human beings are designed to respond to help us to survive and will be explained in much more detail in the next chapter.

Once the terror of my initial response had subsided (after a few hours), I was able to function a bit more rationally at some level. And I needed to be rational because the next day, I had to travel to Devon not to celebrate my son's fortieth birthday, but to respond to his death. A major shift in mindset was called for as I had to make big decisions on the funeral arrangements and manage additional complications. This meant I needed to be fully present and focused in my mind and emotions.

I actually made the choice to do this – I needed to take control of my mind and my thoughts to deal with the powerful emotions I was experiencing. For the next couple of weeks, I put my emotions on hold through the power of mind determination using a variety of tools and techniques and personal spiritual beliefs. I was also kind to myself and gave myself permission to self-soothe, which I will describe in more detail in the next chapter.

Making important decisions

When we are experiencing trauma, we are in a perpetual state of extreme anxiety and stress, so our brains are constantly producing cortisol. This process clouds the mind and causes a sense of confusion and distress, which is why making decisions can be so difficult. To help us cope with that, the brain can choose to put our emotions on hold so that we can focus on the decision-making process and attend to the practical matters following the death of our loved one.

Decisions have to be made to honour our loved one's wishes. These will include executing their will, organising the finances, legal procedures and the funeral – cremation, natural burial or other, arrangements for the ceremony, the after gathering, deciding who or what will be involved. After the initial decisions comes the painful process of sorting out our loved one's personal items. There's so much to consider, so many questions to answer, so much to do.

When our brain puts our emotions on hold so we can deal with the practicalities immediately after losing a loved one, I call this the second stage of shock. Our brain is doing its job by supporting us and numbing our feelings. It's a perfectly natural response at this stage, as it's precisely what we need.

CASE STUDY: SUE

When her husband died suddenly and unexpectedly, Sue couldn't make any decisions. She felt too confused and frightened. Her mind was foggy, her thoughts unclear.

Before her husband had died, it had been he who had made most of the decisions in their relationship, and she was happy for him to do that. Now, faced with the loss of his guidance, she relied on her family and friends to make the funeral arrangements. The only decisions she made were regarding her children's part in the ceremony.

It would help people like Sue if we all talked more openly about death before it happens. There are things I wish I had known when Jack died, like whether he wanted a traditional or natural burial, and what music he would have wanted at his funeral.

I have created a checklist to help you to initiate such discussions with your family and loved ones. Download it free from my website: www.joysackettwood.com

Of course, it helps if your loved one has left a will and personal instructions on how to organise their funeral, sort out their finances and belongings, etc according to their wishes, but in my experience with distressed clients, something is always overlooked. The last thing anyone needs when they've just lost a loved one is for the family to fall out, leading to disagreements which only add to the stress and compound the emotional turmoil for everybody involved. I have known people to fall out so badly over these things that they hold resentment for years and years, which of course creates even more grief and loss.

If there is no formal written evidence of what your loved one wants, and you've never had the conversation with them (as many people haven't), you have to make all of those decisions on their behalf. It will help if everyone who was important in your loved one's life is included and involved in the decision-making experience by having the opportunity to give their input. This way you minimise potential conflicts, as well as your own stress levels because others help and support you during this challenging time and take some pressure off yourself. Even if you are used to being the one leading and in control, this is a time when you will need support.

Support

If you are used to making decisions in business and organising activities, meetings and events, with heightened emotions following a bereavement, your decisions and thinking may be distorted. This is perfectly natural under the circumstances, but you may feel disarmed or disturbed, or even derailed by this. Personally, I certainly did at times. I was also surprised at how some people I thought I knew responded to the death, both on a positive and negative level.

CASE STUDY: LOUISE

When her mother died suddenly, Louise, who owns her own successful business, was absolutely grief stricken. However, as the strong leader in both her family and work life, she found everyone relied on her to continue to organise and make all the decisions and arrangements immediately after her mother's death. They felt that they were unable to help because of the impact of their grief.

Bravely, Louise felt she had no choice but to do her best for her mum, even though the emotional and mental trauma was hard for her to bear.

Everyone who knows your loved one will inevitably be affected by their death, but some responses may surprise, puzzle or even confuse you. You may have noticed how some people show their emotions and some don't. Some people may appear over emotional, while you may think that others don't care at all as they show no emotion. This is probably not the case; it is simply that they haven't been able to process what has happened yet. Just remember that all close members of the family will be experiencing their own emotional responses to shock, death and grief in their own way.

Should you find that some people speak or behave out of character, it helps to know that they are coping with a range of emotions, too. It's important to be aware of this to reduce any potential sources of conflict. It will also help if you need to elicit their support for any reason following the funeral. The time this will take will depend on how close a relationship they had to your loved one. Being aware of your own and other people's responses gives you clearer insight into understanding yourself and others better, which is both educational and empowering.

Mind your own business

It is so important when you're dealing with grief to invest in yourself and become aware of your own emotional needs. Be kind and compassionate with yourself. How else will you manage your work life and be present for the people you love, especially if you have children, husbands, wives or partners to consider? The fact is, you are going through the grief experience together and it will manifest itself in many different ways. How you understand and respond to this unexpected and unwanted experience in your life will help you to cope better under the circumstances.

Your friends, business partners, employees, colleagues, customers and clients – literally everybody associated with you will be affected in some way by your grief experience. This is not intended as judgement, but as a sad fact. Inevitably what happens to you has an impact on others. In extreme cases, this is known as 'secondary trauma' in therapeutic terms. Making considered decisions at this time will be important to avoid misunderstanding and conflict, and if you're not the best placed to make those decisions, I urge you to reach out for support.

PERSONAL EXPERIENCE

The best advice I was given after Jack's unexpected and tragic death was, 'Do not make big decisions for at least six months'. After the funeral, when I returned home to Bournemouth, I really missed the company and comfort of the long-term friends I left behind. They felt so far away from me and I gave serious consideration to moving back and running my business from my hometown in Devon to be nearer to them. In those early stages of my grief, I may well have done it, had it not been for that good advice.

This would not have been a disaster, but it would have meant a lot of organising and planning at a time when any additional stress and strain on myself would not have been wise. Not to mention the consequences of that decision on my loved ones and friendships in Bournemouth. In addition, to re-establish my therapeutic business in Devon would have taken hard work and effort, whereas I had been established in Bournemouth for over a decade.

It is important to be mindful of rash decisions when our emotions are off balance or heightened, as they are in the early stages of the grief process. We need to question ourselves and assess our motives and values. I would not hesitate to give the same advice as I was given to anyone who has just lost a loved one.

Put life-changing decisions on hold for the first six months of your grief. Even if you do decide to make a big decision in your life, delay acting on it for a period of time, at least until your emotions are more settled, so that you are not left with any regrets. This is an essential part of your self-care. Remind yourself that this is a vulnerable time for you.

At work, it may be that you are independent with good managerial skills and leadership qualities, along with a high level of social and communication skills, but even so, it is important to note that at this stage, the emotions involved in grief can distort the thought process. For this reason, enlist support from your partners, colleagues or staff, or even hire a business manager or coach to see you through this major transition in your life.

Grief and work life

The male vs female approach

Grief emotions can be challenging, especially when you're trying to maintain healthy relationships. I have often worked in counselling with successful business-men who struggle with their relationships with wives, partners, children and friends. Often, they are unable to differentiate between family and business life, where the relationship dynamics are completely different. Add grief into the mix and you can end up with a minefield.

Women, on the other hand, even those who are successful in business, are generally much better at balancing work and family life. They tend to be more emotionally connected to their professional life, while men often treat work as a vehicle for making money. Understanding this, depending on whether you are a man or a woman, may well help you to make decisions on how you will continue at work when you are naturally preoccupied by your grief at the loss of your loved one.

If you are able to, step back from your work for a period of time while you come to terms with what has happened to you. There is no set time that you will require as everyone is different. This may take weeks, or it may be months before you feel ready to re-establish yourself in your full-time position again.

___

CASE STUDY: LOUISE

Louise, the successful joint owner of a company in Plymouth with her husband, was able to take as much time off as she needed.

She told me, 'The business was so systemised, and we had a great team in place.'

Although she would usually throw herself into her work and use it as a distraction, she realised that could have had a disastrous outcome on her wellbeing and the business.

'I found giving myself space, removing the usual pressure we put upon ourselves as businesspeople –

the networking, the meetings, trying to tap into every opportunity and be in front of the competition, really helped.'

Female business owners often put a lot of pressure on themselves to prove they can be successful, but businesses eventually need to have their own identities and be able to operate without their founders. As Louise discovered, having a great team and a systemised business is the only way to allow ourselves space when we need it.

CASE STUDY: NIKI

When Niki's grandfather died, suddenly and unexpectedly, she was devastated. They had been extremely close.

'It was the first time someone I loved had died and I felt like my heart had been broken.'

As co-owner of a successful firm based in London, Niki held a key role in a small team of eight staff, so the business struggled when she had to remove herself at such short notice. Luckily, the culture of the business was to support everyone's health and wellbeing, so Niki was able to take time to absorb the shock and return to work when she felt ready to.

I took a step back from working for three months to process my grief while choosing what involvement I did have in my business during that time. Essentially, I took things one day at a time. I knew it was going to be a tough ride, so I decided to accept that and surrender to my grief experience to learn as much as I could from it. Little did I know at that stage just how much I was going to learn.

Suggestions to help you

- Protect yourself at home and at work. Taking care of yourself is so vital at this stage, as this is when you will be at your most vulnerable. In the next chapter, I will offer you tools, techniques and suggestions to help you with this.

- Download a free copy of my Grief Curve from my website, www.joysackettwood.com, and put it somewhere you can see it as a reminder to take care of yourself.

- Download a free copy of the checklist of things that need to be done after a bereavement. www.joysackettwood.com

- Some people will empathise with how you feel, while others won't. Understanding this is important to minimising stress and looking after yourself.

- Some people will respect your feelings and your situation while others will not. It all depends on how emotionally intelligent they are. Sadly, some may even see it as an opportunity to take advantage of your vulnerability, so surround yourself with people you can trust.

- You may need to distance yourself from certain people should their influence prove unsupportive towards you. Do not feel guilty about doing this.

- Reducing any additional source of anxiety or stress right now is your top priority. Be mindful of your own health, physically, mentally, emotionally and spiritually.

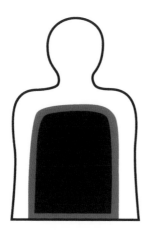

TWO

Building The Second Layer Of RESILIENCE

Education – learning how grief trauma affects your mind, body and emotions.

The second layer of resilience is all about learning. I will help you learn in more detail how trauma and grief affect your brain, influencing your emotions, actions and reactions, and how they affect your body. I will offer you breathing, mindfulness, cognitive behaviour therapy (CBT) and emotional freedom techniques to help you manage this, and teach you how to self-soothe when you need to.

We will look at the power of neuroplasticity, which will help you understand how triggers are significant and unavoidable, and particularly relevant in the grief process. I will then help you to understand the significance of attachment with particular reference to your loved one. Throughout the chapter, I provide explanations, explorations, information and suggestions, sharing techniques which I found helpful at this stage.

How trauma and grief affect our brain

Neuroscience tells us that trauma has a significant impact on us due to the overstimulation of the right side of our brain when it's swamped with naturally produced chemicals such as cortisol. Our right-side brain is our creative side, connected to our imagination, while the left side is the more rational and analytical side.

I have learnt that positive thinking makes positive things happen for us. This is due to the brain producing natural feel-good chemicals such as endorphins and serotonins. With the impact of trauma, our brain and body are flooded with cortisol, causing our emotions to be heightened, hyper-aroused. Under normal everyday threat, such as an unwanted email or difficult customer, this shows up as stress. We are actually designed to cope with small amounts of stress for short periods of time. It's only when we allow stress levels to build up over longer periods of time that it becomes a problem.

Whatever makes us anxious or frustrated can ignite an inner sense of fear or dread. Anything which causes a change in our life can be termed as stress. Even good and positive changes which are for our benefit are stressful as the unknown naturally causes fear, which connects with the right brain. Anxiety is the fear-based emotion connected to stress. This is why, when the trauma of the death of a loved one occurs, our anxiety can feel so powerfully overwhelming.

As you can see on Grief Curve, Diagram 1A in Chapter One, with high levels of anxiety, stress and cortisol flooding our brain, our thoughts become distorted, causing feelings of hyper-alertness and hyper-vigilance. We will feel sensitive at this stage as sleep is often badly affected, finding it difficult to switch off and relax due to being so highly wired.

It is understandable, therefore, that at this early stage of grief, I have often been asked by clients, 'How on earth am I going to cope?'

Memory is all about pattern making by the brain. When we have an experience, it is processed by the brain, and then stored in our subconscious for future reference. Consequently, when we have an experience that is out of our brain's remit, it has no pattern stored in the subconscious.

The forefront of our brain is our conscious self. It is active in the here and now, but is just 10% of our conscious awareness. Since we were born (and even pre-birth), 90% of all of our knowledge and experience has been stored in our subconscious because we have not as yet evolved enough as human beings to store all that knowledge in the forefront of our brains.

Under normal circumstances, we will remember something like crossing the road and nearly getting knocked over, causing us a big fright. The next time we cross that road, we will be extra cautious and remember the previous danger. Eventually, having crossed the road safely a number of times, we'll feel more positive and confident. This is why we teach young children how to cross the road safely – not only to prevent accidents, but also to give them confidence, which in turn reduces stress and anxiety.

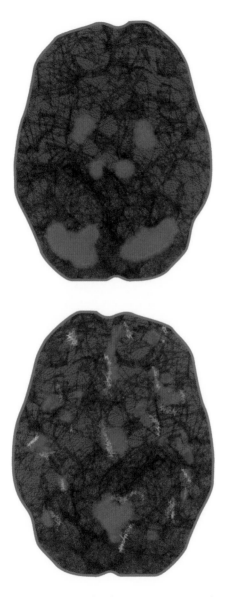

The brain, pre-trauma (top) and post-trauma (bottom)

When we suffer a terrible shock like the death of a loved one, there is no memory to recall. This is a new situation, so the whole of our physical, mental and emotional system is disrupted. The primeval part of our brain – our fight or flight response, which is our inbuilt alarm system inherited from our ancestors – becomes over activated.

How trauma and grief affect our body

When natural chemicals increase our breathing and heart rate, they in turn increase blood flow so more oxygenated blood can be pumped into our muscles, releasing adrenalin into our bloodstream that enables the liver to produce energy-giving sugars, all of which prepares us to fight the threat or run from it. If we are not able to do either of these things, these unnecessary chemicals get trapped in our body, causing high blood pressure and an overworked heart, having an effect on other bodily functions, too, particularly our digestive system. It is not unusual for newly bereaved people to lose their appetite and struggle with tummy upsets.

This is what happened to me – shortly after Jack died, I lost some weight. You may identify with this. Again, taking care of yourself, eating things that you can digest easily at this time, will help keep your physical strength and stamina up.

Loss of sleep is not unusual straight after bereavement, either, as our usual mind and bodily functions have had a big disturbance. This certainly compounds our feelings of emotional distress and unease, so we need to be aware of this and take care of ourselves in every way we can.

Awareness means learning what the signs of stress are in our own bodies. Our bodies communicate to us, but our distracted minds miss the cues. When we feel low in mood, physically and emotionally, we are low in spirit. When we are distressed, our energetic body shrinks (see Layer Eight for more detail). As we are integrated beings, every aspect of our self has an impact on the others. During times of trauma and grief, we need to find ways to raise our energy levels as well as we can to function at the best possible rate.

I suggest four techniques which I personally found really helpful.

Four effective techniques for optimal function

Three-to-five breathing

This is a breathing technique which I have found especially useful, as have many people I have worked with. It serves to intercept the way in which trauma affects the brain and body, enabling us to reduce any uncomfortable feelings and calm our mind, emotions and body. Some people use seven-to-eleven breathing, but I would suggest you see what you are most comfortable with and find what works best for you. In my practice, three-to-five breathing is the most popular.

You simply breathe in through your nose for three seconds and out through your nose for five seconds, keeping your mouth closed. You can also close your eyes when you first start to practise this technique because that will help you to focus without any outside distractions, but soon you will find that you can feel the difference in your body as you become more settled and at ease. Repeat this at least five times, and more if you want to.

This relaxes you quickly because the regular breathing is working with the natural respiratory system in your body, sending a message to your brain to be calm, which in turn calms your heartbeat down to its normal pace. As a consequence, your blood pressure reduces and your pulse rate stabilises, enabling you to feel calmer and more relaxed in your mind, emotions and body.

Mindfulness

This mindfulness technique will help you to reduce any overwhelming panicky feelings on the spot. It quickly engages all your senses and brings you back into the here and now, out of your over-stimulated right brain into your more rational left brain, enabling you to control overwhelming feelings.

First of all, do your three-to-five breathing, completing the inward and outward breaths two to three times. Then open your eyes (if they have been closed while you're doing your breathing), notice one thing in the room/environment and give it your full attention. Notice what you can hear. Notice what you can smell. Notice what you can feel. Touch textures, such as the seat beneath you, with your hands. Enjoy the breeze on your face.

Positive thinking

Cognitive Behavoural Therapy is a positive thinking technique. CBT advocates that our thoughts influence our feelings, which influence the physiology of our body, which then influences our physical action and reactions.

thoughts = feelings = body responses = actions

This is how it works. The brain tunes into any stimulus around and within us. At the speed of lightning, it sends a message to our brain cells and nerve endings, etc, engaging our conscious and subconscious selves. This rush of 'electrons' instantaneously ascertains if the stimulus is a threat or an ally – a friend or a foe.

Our thinking or mental self sends this message to our feelings, known as our emotional or feeling self. In the case of negative stimuli, such as stress and anxiety, our feeling self produces fear-based emotions like worry. These emotions then have an impact on the way the physiology of our body responds to the message, such as in the form of tension – our shoulders and back ache, our chest tightens, our throat dries, our head aches. We may feel fluttering or sickness or tightening of the tummy, etc. Prolonged stress and anxiety is often the root cause of migraines, irritable bowel syndrome (IBS), back problems, heart problems, auto-immune illnesses, etc.

The way our body responds will then have an effect on the way we act physically. That is whatever your own particular coping mechanism may be.

It is logical that when we exchange a negative thought with a positive one, it reverses the response into a more positive experience. We become more present by engaging our left-brain thinking, and by doing this, we take back some power.

There is a lot of power in positive thinking. It naturally boosts endorphin and serotonin levels, which bring you a better sense of wellness. At the same time, do your three-to-five breathing to speed up the change from uncomfortable negative feelings to more comfortable positive feelings.

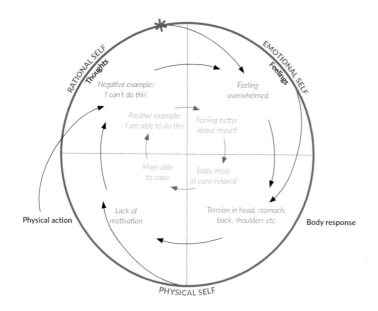

RATIONAL SELF
Thoughts

EMOTIONAL SELF
Feelings

*Negative example:
'I can't do this'*

*Feeling
overwhelmed*

*Positive example:
'I am able to do this'*

*Feeling better
about myself*

*More able
to cope*

*Body more
at ease/relaxed*

Physical action

*Lack of
motivation*

*Tension in head, stomach,
back, shoulders etc*

Body response

PHYSICAL SELF

Cognitive Behavioural Technique

Think of a short positive phrase, known as an anchor, as it grounds you and brings your mind into the present moment, and say it to yourself several times. Examples of positive anchors are 'I am fine' or 'I am OK' or 'I am calm'. Find whatever works for you, but it must start with 'I am...' because you are then owning this positive statement. My anchor is 'I am calm' and I use it with my three-to-five breathing technique whenever I need to, especially when I find myself stuck in traffic. I really don't like being late for appointments!

After using this technique, you will feel calmer and better about yourself because you have been able to change your thoughts positively. Your body will feel more settled, relaxed and at ease, and you will be able to act in a way that is more engaged with what's happening around you. Overall, the process of change speeds up each time you repeat your anchor and engage in the technique, so the rule is practise, practise, practise with repetition, repetition, repetition. The technique and anchor will then become more automatic and empowering each time you need them.

You can use this method whenever you need to, not just dealing with your grief situation in the present, but also way into the future. It will help you whether you are with other people or alone. It will help you to sleep. It will help you deal with difficult people and situations at home, at work and socially.

Emotional freedom techniques

Another great way to gain more control over overwhelming emotions for self-help is the emotional freedom technique (EFT). There is a free video on my website to show you how this works. www.joysackettwood.com

You could train in reiki. This is a natural healing technique that will enable you to perform some self-care which is calming, soothing and relaxing. I explain both EFT and reiki in more detail in Chapter Five.

Science: the power of neuroplasticity

The latest breakthroughs in neuroscience help us to understand how we can overcome negative thinking by building new healthy mental pathways in our brain.

Books have always been my friends. From my humble beginnings, they have helped me to understand life and better myself, so in my deepest grief, it was natural that I turned to books and reading to help me learn about and understand my feelings. The fruits of those learnings, I am now passing on to you.

The best book I have read on this subject is called *The Power of Neuroplasticity* by Shad Helmstetter, PhD.[3]

---

3   S Helmstetter, *The Power of Neuroplasticity: The breakthrough scientific discovery that every thought you think rewires your brain and changes your life* (CreateSpace, 2014)

Helmstetter has written this book in the same way as I approach clinical hypnotherapy sessions with my clients. I often joke that Helmstetter beat me to it and have recommended it to so many people, and I recommend it to you.

It is all about positive thinking and self-talk to retrain our brain to create new neuro pathways to override deeply entrenched negative pathways that have developed over time through repetitive negative self-talk that becomes a habitual behaviour. We are wired to be attuned to threat to survive, so the need to thrive means we must repeat positive suggestions twenty times more often than negative ones to redress the imbalance.

Grieving – for how long?

Grieving is a process of a wide range of emotions, which helps to explain the disturbance you feel when your loved one dies. It takes time to work through those feelings before they settle down and you are functioning at a level that means you can return to life as you know it – although understandably, it will never be the same again without your loved one in it. The lack of their presence in your life will leave a big space, and the strength of the emotional attachment will determine how long you will take before you feel able to face the world.

The minimum time for grief to last is six months. For significant figures in our lives, such as a parent or close grandparent, it can be over two years, and for a beloved husband, wife, partner or child, it can be very much longer.

Triggers

You may find yourself still doing things automatically in the early stages of grief, such as picking up your phone to call your lost loved one at a certain time like you always did before they died. Memory is pattern making, and when the connection to a memory is no longer available, your brain becomes confused as it starts to process the shift in information.

Triggers are things that happen in the present time and remind us of a memory, which we react to as we have an emotional attachment to it.

PERSONAL EXPERIENCE

When I first went to the supermarket after Jack died, I automatically picked up a packet of ginger biscuits which were his favourite. When I remembered he was dead and would never eat them, I burst into tears.

That was a very emotionally painful experience.

CASE STUDY: CATHY

When Cathy's elderly mother died, she had felt she was well prepared for it. Her mother had been suffering from a long-term illness, and Cathy said her death almost came as a relief.

'The grief didn't really hit me big time until I went back to Mum's house in Wales for a Christmas visit to see my nieces. It's the house where I grew up, but because my sister and I had blitzed it while we were there for her funeral, none of her clothes and personal stuff were there. Then it suddenly hit me – she was gone! The house didn't feel like our home anymore and I had to grieve that loss and cry all over again. I actually couldn't stay there for as long as planned because the pain and loss were too much.'

This kind of trigger causes us to swing from one stage of grief to another. Triggers are emotional and painful, especially in the early stages of grief as they catch us out, they're unexpected. When I'm working therapeutically with people, they often talk about triggers in connection to food, music, scents, etc.

Dual process of grief

Gradually, you will find yourself able to function on two levels in a dual process of grief. That is, you continue to process your personal grief while going about your daily activities, engaging in other important relationships, maintaining your professional responsibilities and work commitments. That is why it is so important not only for you to understand what you're going through, but for others around you to understand, too. Grief awareness is essential in mental-health training programmes and to educate therapeutic practitioners, but it is also needed in business support programmes, managerial work and leadership skills training. When a business owner, manager or colleague returns to work following the funeral of their loved one, their grief responses are not over yet. A stepping stone approach back to routine is important to rebuild their sense of purpose.

CASE STUDY: KELLY

When her husband of eighteen years died, my client Kelly felt she was treated well by the corporate employer she worked for. She said they were supportive and compassionate and she felt valued by them. A major contributor to her feeling this was that she had a phased return to work following a period of paid leave.

CASE STUDY: MARY

Mary had a different experience with her employer. She was expected to return to her duties just a week after the funeral of her father, to whom she had been very close, and felt a huge amount of pressure due to her role and the responsibilities she held at work.

Three months later, she became ill and was signed off with stress and anxiety. When she came to me via an employers' assistance programme, it was evident she was experiencing grief. It would have been better for her employers to have understood and supported her appropriately sooner rather than later.

Will I always feel like this?

This is a question I am often asked. What is reassuring is that as we work our way through the grief process, our emotions and what triggers them will become less frequent and intense, and we will be able to enjoy memories of our loved one. They will bring feelings of warmth and fondness rather than upset us.

The intensity of our grief emotions depends on the attachment we had with our loved one. Attachment is an interpersonal bond, and the most intense emotion that arises from the formation of that bond is what is known as 'falling in love', the maintenance of the bond being 'loving someone'. Therefore, the threat of the loss of a loved one arouses anxiety, and the actual loss creates deep sorrow.

In his book *The Other Side of Sadness*, clinical psychologist Professor George Bonanno says it is our capacity to deal with our emotions that enables us to pass through our grief experience to a profoundly new and different sense of meaning in life. His research discovered that some people have more resilience to adversity than others, and this enables them to 'bounce back' from pain and suffering significantly more quickly than others. This resilience, he claims, depends on their life experiences in coping with adversity and manifests itself in their having greater inner strength than others.

While I believe this to be true, I also believe, due to my professional therapeutic experiences, intensive training and work with adult survivors of childhood psychological, sexual, physical and emotional abuse, that resilience can be built and learnt.

Suggestions to help you

- Learn how your brain works.

- Understand the power of your mind.

- Learn how grief can impact you both physically and mentally.

- Self-soothe with three-to-five breathing, mindfulness, CBT and EFT. Practise these methods to help you cope with triggers.

- Become more self-reflective.

- Journal your new learnings, thoughts and feelings.

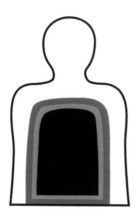

THREE

Building The Third Layer Of RESILIENCE

Surrender – accepting the situation. Making choices, developing the courage and determination to grieve your way in a healthy way.

In building the third layer of resilience, you will understand why surrendering to your grief experience is so important to your wellbeing. You will recognise the complexities of specific challenging grief emotions and how to safely release these, coping with uncomfortable feelings such as guilt and remorse by using sleeplessness productively and creatively. Here I will introduce you to finding meaning within your grief experience, how to make choices that are right for you, and how cultural influences affect your decision making. I will then offer you some ways to bring yourself comfort and suggestions to support you further.

Attend to your grief

PERSONAL EXPERIENCE

Having made the necessary arrangements for my therapeutic business to continue to tick over while I was not as available as usual, I settled myself into the mindset that this phase of my grief would take as long as it needed to take. In surrendering, I worked out that I had enough money to take an extended period out of work if needed and trusted my business would be safe. I told my clients that a close member of my family had died, and they understood and respected my privacy and absence for the initial period of grief.

This took pressure off me and allowed John, who is my business partner and executor, to continue to run the business by dealing with enquiries, emails, managing our website and social media.

If at all possible, I would suggest you approach attending to your grief as taking sick leave. Of course, grief is sickness of the heart, so I suggest you prepare yourself.

Whatever type of business you are in, you will need to protect yourself in case of long-term serious illness or disruption in your life. If you are self-employed, you will need a professional executor to take over your business when you cannot be available. Whether you're producing products or offering a service, you are vulnerable to unexpected disruptions, so allocate somebody to take on your role if need be and take the pressure off yourself.

It is really worth the effort of reviewing your business or employment policy so you know what to do when the need arises. I would suggest everyone, from business owner to contract worker, takes out a bereavement policy with plans in place to help you to cope with traumatic events.

When I talk in terms of plans, I don't just mean regarding work. It is really important to plan funeral and other arrangements in advance so that husbands, wives and partners know your wishes, and you know theirs so you can make measured decisions accordingly during the intense emotions of early bereavement.

Sleeplessness

Guilt keeps you awake at night

As you move through the shock stage of grief, expect a wide range of emotions, including guilt. This manifests as examining yourself and the relationship you had with your loved one. As you can see from the Grief Curve, Diagram 1A in Chapter One, when your feelings start to re-emerge, this is normal.

For many people, ruminating over their relationship with their loved one keeps them awake at night. They may be wondering what they could have done differently, said differently given a second chance. Lamenting is regretting and disappointment.

Guilt can be experienced differently depending on who has died. For example, the loss of an elderly parent is different to losing somebody in their forties. Losing a friend is different to losing a partner or a child. It also depends on the nature of their death. For me, I felt guilty that I had been out of the country when Jack died and couldn't be there for him. Although my rational self knew his death had been unpredictable, the self-deprecating emotions took over. But to mourn is to shed tears over someone, and I did plenty of that.

A period of poor sleep due to overthinking will inevitably happen as it is in the nature of the pain of your loss. This will lead to loss of concentration and appetite, and oversensitivity. As long as this cycle continues, you will experience hypertension, hyper-alertness, hyper-vigilance, none of which is conducive to restful sleep.

It is wise to perceive this phase as a matter of course. Listen to your inner voice while finding a way of getting through it in a healthy way. I found it best not to fight the non-sleeping, getting up in the dark of the night and finding a way to feed my soul and express my inner dialogue.

Find peace with the uncomfortable feelings and concerns regarding your loved one, releasing any guilt or unresolved issues you may be holding. Read, write a letter or a poem to them, journal, draw, paint a picture, play a piece of music you both loved. If you can play a musical instrument, play a song for them; if you can write music, write a song about them. Let go of any bad feelings and find a way to forgive yourself. You may be surprised at the creativity that comes from within you, the gold nuggets that lie within the black nights.

Fear keeps you awake at night, too

You may be kept awake by fears as loss triggers and exaggerates them. For example, you may worry about the possible loss of your business or self-esteem. You may even worry about the loss of sleep itself. If family relationships and friendships have become challenging, the loss of the people close to you can feel threatening, too.

It is helpful to remind yourself that these fears can challenge you under any circumstances, whether you're grieving or not. To help you evaluate these things, be aware you cannot change what has happened or the opinions of others. You can only change yourself.

As the Taoists say, there is yin and yang – a balance – in everything and everyone. Finding and accepting that balance can be a profoundly moving experience.

PERSONAL EXPERIENCE

The first book that I read following the funeral of my son was *Dark Nights of the Soul* by Thomas Moore.[4] As it was a gift, I had no idea how iconic this book is.

I didn't expect to sleep, so I decided to be constructive with my waking time and do whatever felt right to me, and as the author of this book recommends the same thing, I felt reassured that all was well with this approach to grief and distress. I recommend both the approach and the book to you if you are experiencing sleeplessness due to grief.

---

4   T Moore, *Dark Nights of the Soul: A guide to finding your way through life's ordeals* (Penguin Random House, 2004)

I spent the dark hours of the night sitting in my
favourite space, aptly named Peace Haven, enjoying
the quiet, being reflective, thinking about Jack. If I felt
unsure whether I was thinking clearly about any matters
that currently needed my attention, I checked it out
with John.

If you experience any additional challenging emotional
issues in your life during your time of attending to
your grief, you may find it a struggle to navigate them
as you are already in the process of coping with much
distress. Be wise with the expectations of yourself at
this time. Courage will be your strength, so be brave. It
will help you to adapt and cope with your life changes.
Building resilience will allow you to continue in your
life productively and enjoy it as your loved one would
want you to.

Many people believe that if we don't get eight hours'
undisturbed sleep a night, there is a problem, but the
reality is that some people need less or more sleep than
others. Some people are satisfied with six hours' sleep.
Some are refreshed through catnaps for a few minutes
during the day.

We are all unique, and unusual situations result in us
responding in unusual ways at times. Often in the dark
of the night, scholars, poets, writers, artists, composers,
scientists and all manner of gifted and talented people

have found they are at their most inspired, so if you are wide awake at night-time, you are among the best!

Finding meaning

I didn't know where my grief journey was going to take me, but I did know my life was never going to be the same again. It had been changed by the death of my son. But I had survived a lot of adversity in my life and I knew I would survive this one. I was determined it was going to make me a better person. I was determined not to be a victim, not to go down the route of 'Why did this happen to me? Why my son? Poor me'. I would learn and grow through it so it would have meaning for me.

This gave me the power to make choices, even in this powerless situation. It was to my utmost surprise that I was to discover my life had truly changed and taken on a deeper meaning.

In his book *Finding Meaning*,[5] David Kessler added a sixth stage of grief, giving it the same name as the book which he wrote following the death of his son. After the final stage of grief, 'acceptance' according to Elisabeth Kübler-Ross's model, he found a deeper understanding of enriched meaning.

---

5   D Kessler, *Finding Meaning: The sixth stage of grief* (Rider, 2019)

The energy of spiritual realms

I discovered meaning in my grief, too, but for me it went beyond finding meaning to exploring the higher energy of spiritual realms. Grief is the lowest level of energy, and through it, our energetic body literally shrinks, as does our spirit and our soul. To raise our energy frequencies, we need to attend to our grief.

Making good, healthy decisions is our own choice, and knowing we have a choice in extremely challenging circumstances can be a liberating, empowering and settling experience. I read an amazing example of this in a book I would highly recommend, *The Choice* by Edith Eger.[6] The courage and strength of this woman, a Jewish survivor of Auschwitz, cannot fail to inspire and motivate anyone.

Eger tells us of her life. Overcoming the most challenging of adversities, trauma and immense grief, she chose to use her experiences to become an excellent psychotherapist and public speaker to help others. We all have to make choices in life, so making the choice to make good choices is a wise place to begin with. As the popular saying goes, 'Pain is inevitable, suffering is optional'.

---

6   E Eger, *The Choice: A true story of hope* (Rider, 2018)

How your culture influences your grief

Following the early stage of grief, shock, it is important for you to do whatever you need to do to help you cope with your emotions. It will help you here to understand what is shaped by your culture compared to what feels right for you.

I was determined to be assertive in making the arrangements for Jack's funeral. That way, I knew there would be fewer regrets later. I didn't want to just follow the traditional ways of doing things in Western culture; I wanted to take charge of the process and not be afraid to do things differently. I found this hugely empowering and would encourage you to do the same.

In my experience of Western culture, I have found we are generally poor at showing and understanding grief. The stiff upper lip and 'you just have to get on with it' attitude has been the cause of many grief sufferers stuffing their emotions down, only to discover the intensity of these feelings leaking out in situations and manners that make them seem like gross overreactions. Vented in this way, misplaced grief may be perceived as poorly regulated emotions and behaviours, but if our emotions are not allowed to be expressed appropriately and healthily, they may manifest as physical, emotional, mental and spiritual illnesses.

PERSONAL EXPERIENCE

When I was growing up, death and grief were never spoken about. I was aged six when my nan died.
Years later, when I was training in counselling and psychotherapy, I asked my mother why I was never told and why her mother's death had never been discussed. She said that as my nan and I had been so close – we went everywhere and did everything together – she and my dad didn't want to upset me!

Unfortunately, this had a negative impact on me as I was growing up. I had been a depressed child, trapped in unacknowledged grief.

On the whole, my experience of growing up in the British culture was that funerals were always sombre affairs. Everybody wore black, house curtains were drawn to signify that somebody had died in the street where we lived, and we had to go inside or not look as the hearse passed by as a sign of respect. I also remember funerals cost a lot of money in my family. Everyone was buried and there were always family arguments during the proceedings, and afterwards about whose turn it was to tend to the grave and buy the flowers each month. Children were not even considered; they were adult-only affairs. Expressing grief emotions was frowned upon.

George Bonanno in his book *The Other Side of Sadness* shows that cultures around the world express their grief openly through wailing, chanting and engaging in symbolic rituals. People are permitted to show their grief openly, being as vocally expressive as they like for however long they like. He proves that this is a much healthier way for people to grieve, enabling them to be deeply connected with their own emotions while feeling accepted within their communities.

> '...death is not well understood in our culture and learning about your own relationship with it is important before a crisis like this hits you.'
> — Alyss Thomas, psychotherapist

Through studies for my degree in philosophy and theology, I learnt a lot about different world cultures and religions. I went on to teach this fascinating subject from a sociological, philosophical and spiritual perspective at secondary school and sixth-form level for over twenty years. As a consequence, I am well versed in the rituals of dying, death, grief and belief in the afterlife in the many religions, faiths and cultures. I soon became aware of how my culture compared to how I needed and wanted to express my own pain of grief.

Jack's funeral ritual, communal ceremony and various testimonial contributions from family and friends were so important, valuable and significant to me that when I retreated into myself to mourn, I still felt a connection to these significant others. Hence, ritual and ceremony play a vital part in attending to our deeper emotional human needs. This is what some people call the 'spiritual'. Theologians say ritual and ceremony are the outside expressions of what is spiritually happening on the inside.

Everyone has their own particular way of grieving, be it public or private. Some people want and need other people's support more than others. The best thing to do if you find yourself in the position of supporting someone through grief is to ask. Also, ask for the support you need yourself. Often family and friends don't know what to do to help, so they do nothing. This doesn't mean they are ignoring your needs, simply that they are dealing with their own grief, too.

It was my way to retreat into myself. I am by nature introspective and like to retract into solitude, allowing myself to work through my emotions privately. Because of my early years of conditioning, not having or expecting anyone to meet my emotional needs, in my adult years I learnt to do this for myself. I learnt emotional intelligence through educating myself, reading books, studying and observing the wisdoms of others. It is understandable that in the deeply sad place after Jack died, I would respond in the exact same way in solitude.

Give in to expressing your emotions

When I chose to read and learn about what was happening to me, I found it comforting that my grief emotions were validated and understood. You may have experienced how awkward some people feel when you talk openly about grief. A lot of 'protection' happens around grief, people keeping their feelings hidden for fear of upsetting each other. Allowing yourself to go with the flow of your grief, in your private times if need be, will ensure you are meeting your own emotional needs and expressing your emotions as you want to safely, without limits and confinements. Although you may be wise to take a page out of other cultures' books and let it out!

I wrote this poem during a time when the pain of grief felt very raw and physical:

> This Grief
> I feel this pressure
> In my heart it's
> Physical and hot.
> I want it to go away,
> But then I do not
> Lest I forget
> What I forgot
> And now have not.

At that time, my pain seemed to keep my loss alive. I have heard other people say something similar, so I wasn't surprised. Part of me wanted to hold on to it and another part of me needed to let it go. I found myself wailing, crying out loud, making heart-rending noises to bring release.

Wailing may seem to you to be a strange activity, but when the pains of grief came in the early stages, I found it really helpful. Ancient cultures knew this. As vocal noises are vibrations, they are energy frequencies. In some cultures, crying out loud and thumping your chest means setting free the trauma trapped within the body, making it possible to release it via the vibration of sound coming directly out of the body.

Although losing someone you love and care for deeply cannot be 'got over', 'healed' or 'moved on from', the intensity of unattended emotions trapped within the body can hold us back, causing negative disturbances and damaging our quality of life. When we give ourselves permission to acknowledge how we are feeling, we set the intention to give ourselves permission to clear ourselves – release those feelings in a self-care process which is healthy to our general wellbeing. I have created a video using a 'tapping' technique which you can see on my website to help you to do this. www.joysackettwood.com

CASE STUDY: LAURA

Laura's son contacted me initially for an appointment for her. He had become so concerned about her as six years since the death of his father, she still seemed deep in her grief.

When she agreed to see me, she said she felt she couldn't move on with her life because it would be disloyal to her husband, Dave, who had been her partner not only in life, but in business too for over twenty-five years. Following his sudden death, their son Paul seemed happy to take over and run their business. She didn't see the point in getting involved and thought Paul didn't need her help anyway.

After a couple of sessions, she said she was so glad to be able to talk openly about Dave and not have to protect her son's feelings. By the time we finished therapy, Laura was like a new woman. She and Paul communicated honestly for the first time about how things had been for them both since Dave died. Paul had wanted her support in the business and this had been a source of resentment and frustration for him, so Laura enjoyed occupying herself and being involved in business again as she had really missed it.

Laura came to terms with her loss and allowed herself to feel happy again, accepting that this was what Dave would have wanted for her and bringing her a new lease of life.

Memory book

Grief can be exhausting, so occupying yourself with other activities gives your brain and emotions an opportunity to take a break. As well as the activities I have suggested here for you, I made a memory book of my son, which was therapeutic and brought me much comfort.

Sorting through the old photographs was painful, but also joyful, remembering the good times from Jack's childhood and the happier times we had shared. Creating the memory book helped me to express and respond to my own deeper emotional needs, giving me a focus for my grief. By including visual tribute photos, I was revisiting all the times and occasions throughout my son's life that I was connected to. I could feel the strength of that attachment bond, which allowed me to process my grief. Being proactive gave me a sense of power back.

I included everything, from the beginning of his life to the end of my first and second stage of grief. Jack's memory book is also about the planning of his funeral, the arrangements we made, the funeral itself, the gathering of family and friends, and then later, the scattering of his ashes, including photos and images of the whole experience. I wanted to keep a record of the incredible love I felt from those who attended, their contributions and the memories of him that were shared among us.

Making this memory book helped me to purge my feelings and begin to come to terms with my loss. Although it was sad, I found the experience very positive. It meant a lot to me to have evidence that the love and affection I have for my son was experienced by others. Creating something purposeful with meaning gave me comfort and, as I was to discover, much more.

CASE STUDY: LOUISE

When her mum died, Louise's children were devastated. She had been a loving and caring nannie. A friend of hers made the children nannie cushions from her clothes, which they helped to design. This enabled them to feel close to their nannie and comforted them when they missed her.

Some other ways to comfort yourself:

- Eat favourite 'memory foods' on specific days or occasions
- Create a photographic collage
- Plant your loved one's favourite flowers
- Visit their favourite places
- Wear a particular scent
- Listen to particular music for comfort and connection

- Write poetry

- Keep a journal of your feelings and emotions

PERSONAL EXPERIENCE

When I was selecting the photographs and images to glue into the memory book, I was planning to include a picture of a sculpture that John and I had come across on social media called 'Melancholy' by Albert Gyorgy which accurately expressed the way I felt at that time. The copper sculpture was a seated figure on a bench slumped over with a large hole where the body should be, representing the intense sadness and emptiness felt when somebody dear to us dies. For me, as a parent grieving for the loss of my child, it was a really powerful, thought-provoking, emotive image.

The picture was on the table with other photos to be sorted into order ready to be glued into the book. While John and I sat there talking over a cup of tea, the picture suddenly flicked up and fell from the table. We looked at each other in complete surprise and were even more astonished when we searched for it everywhere. The picture was not on the floor – it couldn't be found. A complete mystery.

After a while of trying to make sense of it, John went to fetch a torch and returned to shine the light through a small crack in the floorboards. And there was the picture. Not only had it fallen unaided from the table, but it had landed at exactly the right angle to go straight through the narrowest of cracks. We knew immediately that it was Jack telling us he really didn't want that picture in his book.

To me, the message was loud and clear: 'Please do not grieve, Mum.'

I responded by saying out loud, 'I am a human being and I will attend to my grief as well as I can. I will surrender to it so that we can move on in our new and different relationship. But of course, I will always miss you in the physical world.'

That incident was to change the course of my life and be the inspiration for this book.

It was later on in my grief journey that I came to understand the full meaning of why my son didn't want me to remain in the pain of suffering. I look forward to sharing this with you.

Suggestions to help you

- Allow yourself to surrender and let go of your emotions

- Consider how your culture influences your grief experience

- Choose some ways to comfort yourself

- Consider what the meaning within your grief experience may be

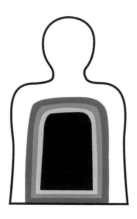

FOUR

Building The Fourth Layer Of RESILIENCE

I nitiate – strategies to help you cope, using initiative and understanding, and supporting self, family, friends, colleagues, staff, employees, etc.

In this fourth layer of resilience, you will learn to cope in all areas of your life. You will explore how to initiate strategies to help you financially, whether you're in employment or run your own business, to reduce stress and anxiety. You will look at how to support others – family, friends and colleagues – while grieving yourself. You'll see why specialist grief counselling is important, learning why anger is a key emotion in grieving, and the dynamics of anger, remorse and regret. You'll discover unhealthy and healthy ways to cope with difficult feelings, and the differences between men and women when it comes to seeking help and expressing anger. Then I will offer you suggestions to help raise your positivity and natural energies.

Strategies to help you cope financially

When I had the 'flying photo' experience while I was creating my memory book for Jack, I got the sense that my son didn't want me to stay in the pain of my grief because of the damaging impact it would have on me. He knew how it would interfere with my business, my financial livelihood and my therapeutic service to others, which I see as my life's purpose.

If you are self-employed like me, you may be solely responsible for your financial income. Where there's no sick pay or holiday entitlements, this can put a lot of pressure on you to meet your and your family's needs. If you have a business partnership, you may have some kind of financial cushioning should you need to take time off work. Either way, it is always wise to have money put aside for unforeseen circumstances, but of course, the extent to which you can do so depends on the level of income you have.

I am fortunate to have a small teacher's pension which covered me taking time off from my work and business. Without such provision, you may need to apply for government assistance or a loan to tide you over until you feel ready to resume your work.

If the nature of your business requires face-to-face work with clients, you will need to respond to this situation – giving yourself time and permission to attend to your grief – sooner rather than later. Arranging to cover yourself financially as quickly as possible, or even better before the situation arises, will at least take some of the stress and anxiety levels off you.

As you are now moving through the Grief Curve, Diagram 1B, you will have your up and down days as your emotions swing between the stages. Hopefully, by now you will be able to recognise this and be compassionate with yourself. You will find that managing and regulating your own emotions is one thing, but if you have children and close family also affected by the loss of your loved one, your own grief becomes more complex.

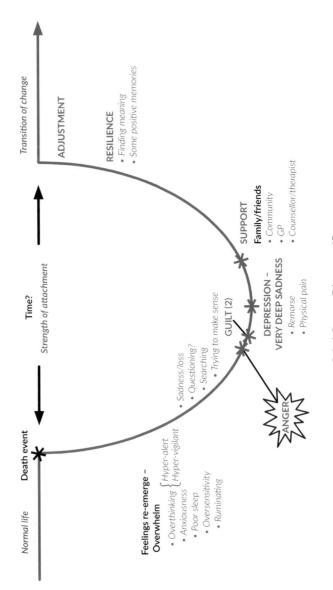

Normal life

Transition of change

Death event

ADJUSTMENT

Time?

↑ *Strength of attachment* ↓

RESILIENCE
• *Finding meaning*
• *Some positive memories*

Feelings re-emerge –
Overwhelm
• *Overthinking* {*Hyper-alert* / *Hyper-vigilant*}
• *Anxiousness*
• *Poor sleep*
• *Oversensitivity*
• *Ruminating*

• *Sadness/loss*
• *Questioning?*
• *Searching*
• *Trying to make sense*

GUILT (2)

SUPPORT
Family/friends
• *Community*
• *GP*
• *Counsellor/therapist*

DEPRESSION –
VERY DEEP SADNESS
• *Remorse*
• *Physical pain*

ANGER

Grief Curve, Diagram 1B

Supporting others – family and friends

Managing other people's emotions, especially in close relationships, as well as your own is a high expectation. There's often a perceived need for protection around grief and the grieving. I would strongly recommend family counselling – this way everyone will get the support they need rather than each worrying they are upsetting the others.

Specialist grief counselling enables you to understand what is happening to you and what other members of your family and friends need. Many people I have worked with therapeutically are surprised when they come to me for grief counselling at the full implications, dynamics and complexities of grief.

Good role modelling

If you initiate therapeutic support for yourself, others will likely see you as a role model.

CASE STUDY: JULIETTE

When Juliette first came to see me, she was really struggling with her children's grief as well as her own. She just didn't know how she was going to cope. Aged fourteen and sixteen, her children couldn't deal with the sudden death of their father on top of school and college work. They certainly couldn't deal with their mum's grief while they needed her love and support for their own grief.

Through the therapy Juliette and I did together, she learnt a lot about grief. Becoming stronger and more resilient as a result, she was able to support her children appropriately to express their feelings. In other words, she became an excellent role model.

Dealing with others' grief as well as our own is challenging. When it involves children, we are naturally wired to be more protective and defensive, so it's a tricky balance to manage.

Supporting others in business/at work

If you attend grief counselling, you will be in a better position to support your employees, staff or colleagues should the need arise in the future. Taking care of yourself is a top priority. By accepting individual and business support, you are showing your initiative to lead yourself through this difficult time with flying colours. Your business relationships will thank you for being wise and attuned to your own and your business needs in a positive way.

If you run your own business and don't have an executor, now is a good time to employ a business coach or manager to support you and your business through this period of your life. Taking the initiative in this way makes sense as you will then have no regrets to look back on in the future, knowing you have done the best you could in a difficult situation. All successful businesspeople are aware that reaching out for support shows strength and courage, not weakness. Investing in advice from experts is a positive thing to do, relieving you of stress and strain at a difficult time.

Employers' assistance programmes

Many corporate businesses now offer counselling to their staff, which can be accessed through Human Resources. Often clients come to me through referrals in which six sessions are paid for by the company. If this is not enough, then they may continue to see me, paying for themselves.

Some businesses are supportive in other ways. With long-term leave, some will offer a staggered back-to-work package to ease employees back in. Other employers have been less compassionate and expect employees to return to normal work shortly after the funeral of a loved one.

Returning to work too quickly after bereavement is never a good idea. You will not be able to remain focused for long periods of time and are unlikely to be fully productive in your role. Unfortunately, some employers refuse to recognise this, which is usually counterproductive as it creates problems at work and extends the grief process. If your employer is less than sympathetic, I would advise you to start job hunting as soon as you're back on your feet.

Specialised grief counselling

Our culture is only just coming to terms with the value of professional counselling and therapeutic support. It was once considered a failure of some kind with a stigma attached to 'not being able to cope by yourself', but the recent media exposure, thanks mainly to the Duke and Duchess of Cambridge's Heads Together charity and the Duke and Duchess of Sussex's charitable activities, has promoted mental-health issues in the public's consciousness. Prince Harry's Invictus Olympic Games for military veterans was a great start in underlining the importance of acknowledging Post Traumatic Stress Disorder (PTSD) and the impact of trauma on people's mental health and quality of life.

With the COVID-19 outbreak, we saw the upsurge of National Health Service (NHS) key workers being offered free professional online counselling support. I was a volunteer in this support as the nation recognised the mental and emotional trauma of working intensely on the frontline against a highly contagious virus. Professional support is finally being acknowledged as a positive action rather than the old-fashioned 'just get on with it' approach.

Can grief be healed?

It is important to emphasise here that grief cannot be healed. Grief is not an illness you can recover from; it is an altered state of life that you learn to accept over time. Your life will go on, but it can never be the same as it was.

In my private counselling practice, clients have told me that when people comment on them 'getting over their loss', they actually feel offended. The loss of a loved one will always be present in their lives. They will hold their loved one in their heart; I simply help clients reduce the pain of their loss and come to enjoy life more.

Should anyone suggest you can be healed of your grief, it would be wise to be cautious. Energy therapies such as reiki and EFT will help you to reduce tension, calm and relax you. As a professionally qualified and experienced practitioner in both these modalities myself, I would say that, especially in the early stages of grief, counselling – that's talking therapies, complemented with some gentle energy healing – can really help.

CASE STUDY: MARIANNE

When Marianne first came to see me, she felt that there was no future at all. Even though she had children, the death of her husband was so overwhelming that she couldn't even imagine being happy or enjoying life again. Her husband's death made her realise how much she had relied on him, making her feel totally helpless in his absence.

We worked using the Grief Curve, which she found incredibly helpful. She said, 'I have learned from the Grief Curve and the effect of trauma on the brain, understanding this has really helped me to heal.' Marianne learned to accept that grief is something we never get over but learn to live and cope with the new situation.

She found the confidence to make changes in her home, family and work life. Her sessions taught her to accept her situation and live as a family of three instead of four. She did come to enjoy Christmas surrounded by her family which she initially never thought possible.

Women vs men in counselling

Statistically, there is still evidence that women will attend counselling to talk about their feelings more than men, although I have personally seen a rise in the number of men attending my private practice in the past few years. Again, I believe this is due to a positive shift in social media influences promoting the 'new man image', which we are beginning to enjoy more in our Western society. Men getting in touch with their feelings are being promoted as sexy and glamorous. Each generation paves the way for new ways of doing things, and going on previous stereotypical male attitudes, this can only be seen as a positive.

Men now are generally more 'hands on' with bringing up their children than previous generations, being in touch with their feminine side. The choice to have fewer children probably helps, but it is still the females who are the main care givers in our society as we women are biologically built to be the nurturing primate of our human kingdom. Consequently, when there is the loss of a loved one in the family, it is still generally the woman who will be the go-to for love and comfort.

CASE STUDY: ROSIE

When Rosie's daughter died, she became the main carer of her grandchildren aged eleven and five. Her own plans to develop her business had to be put on hold. Now, four years later, she feels ready and able to resume some of her business ideas while continuing to raise her daughter's children.

Anger

Anger features significantly on the Grief Curve. When a loved one dies, especially if it is an unexpected death, it is not unusual to feel angry, generally at the injustice of the situation and the loss of the important person in our life. A major aspect of the grief process is anger, and it is recognised that men and women generally express anger differently.

Male vs female anger responses

Even before I became a professional counsellor, I was aware of the different ways in which males and females express anger due to my career as a secondary school teacher. Boys would show their anger outwardly in physical form by fighting to resolve differences, while girls would generally shout at each other and argue, or stay silent and keep it in.

From a young age, boys tend to be given permission to express anger, while girls are told it is not what 'nice girls do'. On the other hand, girls are allowed to cry, while boys are taught it's not what 'big boys do'. As much as we think these attitudes have changed in our modern society, in reality, they still remain. Most fathers want their boys to stand up for themselves, to look after themselves if they're attacked, while they tend to treat their daughters like delicate little princesses. The message comes across loud and clear that anger is OK for boys, but not for girls.

This is reflected in my counselling practice. The majority of men who attend are wanting to deal with an anger problem as they have realised it's having a negative impact on their marriages and relationships. I have seen many angry men who, when given the space and safety, can express a wide range of emotions and learn better communication skills.

With grief, anger affects both men and women alike. When counselling women, I help them to express their anger in the safety of an accepting, non-judgemental environment. Often women can feel disturbed by the intensity of the anger they feel.

Moral anger

At the root of our anger in grief is a sense of injustice, feeling wronged, unfairness, something taken out of our control and imposed upon us. When our loved one dies, this is how it feels.

You may find yourself asking why this has happened, and why it has happened to you. You may not be able to find sensible, rational answers to your questioning. You may even feel angry with your loved one for leaving you to cope with life without them.

This is something I have often heard married people or those in long-term relationships say when their partner has died. Anger is a perfectly normal emotion that we all feel on a daily basis, but when it comes hand in hand with grief, we often feel guilty about feeling it as we think it is not the 'right' or 'respectful' thing to do.

Guilt, as Diagram 1B shows, almost always comes in the second stage of grief when the realisation of your loved one's death sinks in. They really have gone from this physical life and there's nothing you can do about that. It is out of your control.

It is interesting that I have experienced a gender reversal with grief. Men, who generally express their anger so readily, will tend to suppress this emotion when they're grieving until it manifests itself in other ways. Women, on the other hand, will want to talk openly about feeling angry.

CASE STUDY: CHRIS

Chris was experiencing problems in his relationship with his fiancée. He told me his father had died when he was sixteen and his mother remarried just two months later. Chris didn't realise how angry he had been back then until he acknowledged that he felt 'this man' had taken advantage of his mother's vulnerability.

Fast forward ten years and Chris has come to realise via therapy that he was venting his anger at his mother for remarrying and projecting it on to his fiancée. Once he worked this through, along with his anger at his dad for 'leaving him', Chris enjoyed a much happier relationship with his fiancée.

Dynamics of anger

When an angry person is feeling this strong emotion, they are hurting on the inside. Someone lashing out, either physically, emotionally or verbally, is expressing this hurt. Of course, it is inappropriate to take anger out on others or damage property. People generally feel threatened by anger when it is expressed aggressively. The silent person tends to be more able to contain their anger, but the lowest place in the Grief Curve, Diagram 1B is depression, which is associated with unexpressed anger.

Talking about your anger is important to your health and self-care. Acknowledging that you feel angry is adult, showing emotional intelligence, but people often say they are afraid to talk about anger as they may be judged by family or friends. Talking your anger through with a professional non-judgemental counsellor will likely be the best way to support yourself.

Anger as remorse and regret

Sometimes people feel angry with themselves for personal reasons, which are often the cause of regret and remorse. There may have been unresolved issues between you and your loved one, so you now believe the opportunity to resolve them has gone. The inner conflict of regret can keep you awake at night.

The most important thing is to understand this is normal. Anger is a normal stage of grief. What is vital is to allow yourself to face anger with courage. Be brave about it. Really explore the reason for your anger.

Overcoming anger

Just as you can find the compassion to forgive others, you need to show yourself compassion and forgive yourself. It will help to ask yourself whether your loved one would want you to treat yourself badly. Probably not – they loved you, so they would want you to be kinder to yourself and let whatever is making you angry go.

From your anger, you can learn what would be the best way to honour the memory of your loved one. This is explained well in a deeply spiritual book by Matt Kahn, *Everything is Here to Help You*.[7] If you face up to uncomfortable feelings, they will hold a good purpose for you. It is really important to initiate your own self-care.

PERSONAL EXPERIENCE

My greatest source of remorse, regret and anger was around the fact I was away on holiday, not even in the country, when my son died. It pained me so much to think of him on his own. After all, I'd had the honour and privilege to be there for my mother when she died in hospital. I had kept her company, holding her hand, until the moment she stopped breathing and I felt her soul leave her body.

---

7   M Kahn, *Everything is Here to Help You: A loving guide to your soul's evolution* (Hay House, 2018)

But I had not been there for my son. The thoughts and images of him dying alone kept me awake at night. It was so hard for me to get my head around. I wondered how it must have been for him, what death was like for him and how he experienced it.

Following one sleepless night, I was sitting in my cabin quietly meditating when I had a remarkable experience. I got a strong sense of Jack 'telling' me to look in my drawer in the cupboard and 'get my swingy thing out'. What he was referring to, I was astonished to discover, was my crystal pendulum, put there two years previously when John had built the cabin. I'd never used it and had little interest in it, and had completely forgotten about it.

The purpose of a pendulum is to talk to a spirit, asking closed questions so it can give answers – yes or no depending on the direction it swings. After asking an obvious question to determine the yes and no swing direction, I decided there would be no harm in going along with the suggestion.

I tentatively asked, 'Are you OK?' An emphatic yes came in reply. Wow, that was a relief!

I went on to ask Jack about his death. He told me he didn't realise he'd died at first as he felt no pain at the moment of his death. Then he could see his own body. He was met by family members, Nanny Wood and Nanna, my mum and ex mother-in-law. He was really doing well and was happy.

Eventually, when I asked Jack for his forgiveness for not being there for him, the pendulum moved quickly, forming the shape of a cross. In my heart and spirit, I knew he had drawn a kiss – this was my son 'telling me' he loved me and all was well.

I felt such a great sense of peace and comfort. My son had found a way to communicate with me and help me – and this was just the start of our new relationship.

In truth, it still took me a little while to forgive myself. Again, it happened in meditation when my son reminded me that he had done things that needed my forgiveness when he was living in the physical world. By this time, I was writing down what I 'heard' from him. On this occasion, this is what he told me:

'Anger is the opposite to love. It is pain, it is hurt. To get even, to un-forgive, to abuse, to violate the rights of others, to be mean, to be spiteful, to be alone, to be fearful, to be sad, to grieve, to be isolated.

'Love is real, love is all, love is truth and light. Anger is darkness, soul draining. Love is soulful, full of love. This is why anger must be addressed, resolved, made good. Anger has a purpose – it is here to help you learn. It is part of your soul's evolution.'

Here are some ways people will try to block out anger and challenging emotions. These are all low-energy/ negative activities:

- Drinking too much alcohol

- Smoking

- Taking drugs

- Social media obsession

- Casual sex/porn

- Over- or under-eating

- Eating too much sweet and sugary food

- Gambling

- Overspending

- Over cleaning/tidying their home

All of these are ways to:

- Fill the void – the hole you feel inside you

- Push down uncomfortable feelings

- Distract yourself

- Comfort yourself

- Dull the pain of the loss of your loved one

- Cope with the sadness and the loneliness you feel

It may seem obvious to say that in the long term, these activities, which are quick-fix coping mechanisms, will become a serious problem. As a professional, I am aware that many addictions can be traced back to the sufferer originally using a quick fix to help them cope with the difficult feelings following the loss of a loved one, but all these do is drain you of your energy and weigh you down. With this awareness, you will hopefully be better placed to find healthier ways of coping with challenging emotions.

PERSONAL EXPERIENCE

When Jack died and I was coping with the initial shock and early stage of grief, I had a few cigarettes. I smoked when I was younger, eventually giving up, but whenever I am deeply emotionally upset, like when I got news of the death of my dad and my brother, and when my mother died, I will have a cigarette. I am not proud of it, but I know I will always stop again once I feel less vulnerable and emotionally overwhelmed.

There are many healthy, positive high-energy strategies that have helped me cope. Here are a few favourites:

- Walking in nature
- Writing
- Journalling
- Meditation
- Visualisations
- Dancing

- Exercising

- Sourcing good, wholesome, nutritious organic foods

- Cooking/experimenting with new recipes

- Reading

- Painting/decorating

- Arts and crafts

- Revisiting loved hobbies

- Singing

- Music

- Uplifting films/videos

- Comedy/laughter

- Spending time with positive, supportive people

- Spending time with children

- Spending time with animals and pets

Be careful of the busy-bee syndrome, which can also be used as a distraction from feeling your emotions. During the grief process, it's great to be both active and reflective. Be kind to yourself. The activities I have listed are all energy boosting because they engage your brain in a constructive way. Positive activity boosts the natural endorphins and serotonins in your brain, which produce feelings of health and wellbeing.

It's important, then, for you to initiate these activities for yourself.

The science of positivity and wellbeing

CASE STUDY: NATURE WALK

I remember watching a documentary on TV about a controlled scientific experiment involving two groups of volunteers. They were older people who frequently experienced low moods.

Prior to the experiment, the volunteers were each given the same test to complete about their low moods, and given a score. Then the researchers took a brain scan of each volunteer before the experiment took place.

The volunteers were divided up into two groups. One group was asked to meet up and play table tennis three times a week, while the other group was asked to meet up and go for a twenty-minute walk together in nature. After six weeks, they were asked to return to the test centre to discuss their experiences.

All the people taking part agreed that they had enjoyed the social aspect of their activity. The people in the table tennis group said that learning a new skill had improved both their physical and mental coordination, and was fun. The people in the walking group said how relaxing it had been talking together while walking.

All the volunteers were given the same written test as they had done at the start of the experiment. The results showed that they all felt more positive. To identify which group had progressed more in positivity – the one playing tennis or the walking-in-nature group – they were then given another brain scan.

Interestingly, the results showed that the people who walked in nature had raised their positivity more. While it was clear that the social aspect of both activities was a factor in raising everyone's positivity – all of these people said they felt happier for choosing to take part in the experiment and good about the positive results – the actual activity of walking in nature was identified as bringing about the most significant change in the volunteers' brains.

This can be seen as evidence for taking the initiative to engage in something new and different, promoting positivity, self-care and self-nurturing.

During the COVID-19 lockdown, many people came to realise how enjoyable walking, cycling, running and exercising outdoors in nature is. By reconnecting with nature, listening to the natural sounds of birdsong, water flowing, the buzzing of insects, smelling the flowers and fresh air, generally taking life at a slower pace, we can all take the initiative to do something that has been proven to be positively uplifting.

Suggestions to help you

- Reduce any work-based stress and anxiety areas quickly and effectively.

- Work through difficult emotions with a professional counsellor.

- Be kind and compassionate with yourself.

- Choose from the list of positive high-energy activities to try out.

- Enjoy positive companionship.

- Walk in nature – regularly.

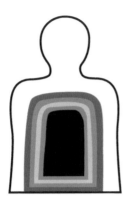

FIVE

Building The Fifth Layer Of RESILIENCE

L ove – self-love, self-nurturing, taking care of yourself.
This is all about making healthy choices for your
own wellbeing so you are able to love and care for
others and your business/work life.

Following on from the previous level about initiating
positivity, this level will delve deeper into understanding why self-love and self-nurturing are so important
to your health and wellbeing, especially while you're

grieving. You will learn how to cope with any additional pressures within relationships and how these may affect you, and how to develop and enjoy emotional intelligence. You'll understand the complexities of self-image and create a positive one for yourself.

In addition, you will come to understand yourself as an energy being and what this means to you. Then I will explain some holistic therapies that will help comfort you. In this way, I hope you will feel able to start to move through the Grief Curve, Diagram 1B, gaining some empowerment over the situation you have found yourself in since the death of your loved one.

Self-love

To support you further in your process of learning to live with painful grief, I offer you my LOVE model which encompasses the layers of the RESILIENCE model like an affectionate hug. My intention is that by the time you have completed this book, you will be:

- **L**earning, getting to know yourself through your grief

- **O**ptimistic, becoming positively enlightened and strengthened by your grief journey

- **V**ictorious, as you will feel you have conquered emotional challenges and accomplished a positive outcome

- Evolving, as you continue to transform yourself and your life on every level, emotionally, mentally, physically and spiritually

This means that setting the intention to love yourself will have positive impacts on those you care for, in addition to making you a Shining-Light example of courage and inner strength. Therefore, shifting from loss to gain.

Right now, you can make the choice to love yourself. Choose to love yourself unconditionally as you loved the precious person who has gone from your life. That means accepting yourself with all your imperfections.

To be able to do this, you must silence the critical inner voice which keeps telling you that you have to be perfect to be loveable. So many people, especially women, give up on themselves because they feel flawed in some way.

Again, this behaviour can be traced back to early childhood conditioning from parents, environment, social status, schooling, cultural and religious beliefs, leading to you feeling you have to seek acceptance and approval to feel loved. But the most important relationship we have is with ourselves.

Why self-love is so important

People often misunderstand the concept of self-love, thinking it to be a notion of arrogance, conceit and egotistical beliefs. If we are completely and totally selfless without consideration for our own needs, we are in danger of adopting a martyr mindset or victim mentality, which is disempowering.

Women especially need to be cautious as we tend to grow up with romantic ideas of what love is. Even after decades of equal rights changes for women, within the Western world, there are still social expectations and pressures placed upon us, expecting us to put others before ourselves. For women in cultures with less equal treatment, this is an ongoing battle which permeates every aspect of their lives. Sometimes this may be appropriate, but generally, we all need to take care of our own needs before anyone else's.

There are different types of love. There is the love we have for our husbands/ wives/ long-term partners, love for our family, love for our children and love for our friends. We can include love for our pets, too. Throughout the ages, artists, poets, writers, etc have all attempted to express and define what love is. To me, I would define love as 'perfect understanding'. This includes not just others, but understanding of ourselves, too.

What is healthy self-love?

Healthy self-love is accepting and knowing there is no need for perfection. In grief, someone with a healthy self-image will cope better than those without. They are authentic; their mind is not distracted by keeping up an unrealistic self-image. They are free to enjoy a balanced lifestyle of work and activities, are emotionally stable. In touch with their feelings, they can experience both the painful ones and the joyful ones. They are aware of the importance of their own self-care and kind to themselves.

Knowing their limits and personal expectations as well as setting achievable goals and challenges appropriate to the situation, they have healthy values, take reasonable care of their appearance and attend to physical, psychological and spiritual needs. Aware of their own emotional needs, they are able to attend to them and get them met, too. They have self-respect and set healthy boundaries with others. Having done their 'inner work', they are confident. They enjoy an inner strength that is resilient and have a good relationship with themselves. In grief, they can therefore adapt quickly to change.

All this is also known as having emotional intelligence.

Grief is an opportunity to develop emotional intelligence

Emotional intelligence is so important, especially while we're grieving, but it is something that many of us didn't learn well while growing up. This is mainly due to having passed our formative years in an era when emotions were not generally expressed or understood, which is what happened to me. Going through the Grief Curve, Diagram 1A helps clients in the early stage of grief to identify the range of emotions that they will experience, and many more besides. Through my work with grieving clients, I have come to believe grief is an opportunity to develop our emotional intelligence and improve our relationship with ourselves.

The Greek philosopher Aristotle said, 'Knowing yourself is the beginning of all wisdom.' Indeed, all therapeutic counselling is about learning emotional intelligence, and becoming more reflective and insightful as a result. We also become more self-aware and self-knowing, which is empowering, making us resilient, able to cope with whatever life challenges come our way.

Here is a good example:

CASE STUDY: ROSA

Rosa, a Doctor of Psychotherapy, trainer and supervisor, believes she was able to cope with the death of her beloved brother three years ago because of her developed emotional intelligence and inner resolve. She had cared for her brother, who had been affected by cerebral palsy since birth, and her commitment to caring for him as well as her own five children while running her busy counselling business is a shining example of love and dedication in action.

On coping with her grief, she told me, 'Somehow, I managed to continue with my practices and didn't postpone any appointments. Looking back at those days and weeks, I am surprised at my professionalism and ability to put aside my own feelings and enter the world of my clients.'

As you become more aware of the consequences of the decisions and actions you take, you will naturally start to make healthier choices. You will find that you become less critical of others, less judgemental and more tolerant. As a reflection of accepting yourself, you will be accepting of others. In other words, you come to love yourself.

This spirit of self-compassion is called 'Maitrī' in Buddhism, knowing that we are not perfect. The more considerate we become towards ourselves, the more considerate we become towards others, and vice versa. In grief, we must be considerate towards ourselves.

Be kind, nurture, care for and love yourself.

PERSONAL EXPERIENCE

I knew I had to take care of myself when Jack died. From experience, I realised how the death of a loved one can change people adversely, especially how mothers struggle with the loss of their child in a way a childless woman cannot comprehend. My own mother told me she could never come to terms with the death of my brother. To raise a child from a baby to adulthood, and then have them die before you is devastating.

This is why I became determined to learn from the experience, rise above it and see how I could better help others through it.

Grief and coping with adversity

Grief can compound any existing pressures in relationships. In your family, there may be someone who is susceptible to overusing substances or destructive behaviours to help them escape uncomfortable or painful feelings, so grief could be a time of particular danger for them, adding pressure on you.

Addictions are toxic, having a negative effect on all members of the family. They destroy relationships. I would strongly suggest you get appropriate help and free support from Alcoholics Anonymous (AA), Narcotics Anonymous (NA) or Gamblers Anonymous (GA) if you or someone you love is suffering from such an addiction. You can find local family groups to attend, online meetings or Facebook groups for pretty much any destructive behaviour.

If you are in a relationship that is abusive, you could find your grief harder to bear as you are already coping with a complicated emotional situation. Abuse recovery programmes teach disempowered women and men to know their personal rights, respect themselves, be assertive and not allow others to treat them disrespect-fully. This is the beginning of self-love, which is what I learnt while recovering from the adverse effects of my first marriage.

Sadly, from my experience, many families are affected by substance abuse and/or violence within the home due to the dynamics associated with grief. There are support groups that meet locally and online and are free to join. You can find them via a Google search.

Why you may find self-love challenging

As you work through your process of grief, the way in which your family role models dealt with this issue will have an impact on how you will deal with it. You will have a blueprint of what constitutes acceptable and unacceptable behaviour, creating your belief systems.

As a result of this early conditioning, some of us, particularly women, don't understand the meaning of healthy self-love. We may have heard of it, but we don't believe it applies to us, or how it applies to us.

This is what I discovered for myself many years ago, and I still come across it with people I help with poor self-esteem and self-confidence. And grief compounds any existing feelings of loss or lack.

Self-nurturing therapies

Part of my own self-care was to enjoy therapy sessions. By its nature, grief can drain us of our energy, and so engaging in self-nurturing therapies will help to restore us.

Alongside the suggestions I have made so far in this book, there are therapies that will help you to raise your energies if you are feeling lethargic. While talking therapies such as grief counselling will help you to explore your feelings and experiences of grief, natural-energy therapies such as reiki, HypnoReiki™, EFT and hypnotherapy will help you to improve your energetic body, enhancing your physical, emotional, mental and spiritual wellbeing.

A brief history of energy healing

The idea that we are energy beings who possess personal energy both within us and surrounding us is nothing new. Neither is the idea that our personal energy can move and create wellness. Throughout history, different cultures have known and developed this, and benefited by tapping into it while working with it in different forms.

The tradition of energy healing can be traced back at least 5,000 years in Eastern medicine, but it's probably much older. Cave paintings in central China, which are thought to depict ancient healing methods similar to those still used today, have been carbon dated as being around 6,000 years old.

The basic concept is that we are all made from energy, as are all living things. It follows, then, that if our energy is depleted or out of balance, it will cause us a problem.

Qigong (with its later derivative tai chi), yoga and acupressure (the forerunner of acupuncture) can all be traced back 5,000 years, before which there is little written evidence. While yoga and qigong are accepted in the West as forms of exercise, these were first developed as healing treatments, having a deep effect on our internal energy.

Reiki was founded much later, although the basis of the method was developed by Dr Mikao Usui from documents dating back to the seventh century, which were brought to Japan from Tibet. After many years of translating and studying these documents, Dr Usui began practising and refining his reiki system in the poor district of Kyoto, before moving to Tokyo to open his first clinic and teaching school in 1921.

Energy healing works by making any necessary adjustments to the flow of energy around the body, releasing blocked energy, stimulating the flow where it is weak or regulating it where there is too much. Balance is the key to good health. It is also common practice to clear out used energy to allow new energy to flow into a body to maintain good balance.

It is only in recent decades that energy work has emerged in the West. Energy practices and therapies such as reiki, yoga and acupuncture have become more acceptable within the medical/science community as ways of helping promote relaxation, calmness and wellbeing, and are available in some hospitals and cancer support units.

Auras

Throughout the centuries, some people have claimed to be able to see energy, also known as auras, appear as layers of various colours around the body. But it wasn't until the twentieth century that a scientist actually proved it.

In 1939, Semyon Kirlian accidentally discovered that if an object on a photographic plate is connected to a source of high voltage, an aura or corona of electrical discharge can be photographed. This discovery finally proved the existence of an aura, or bio-energy field as it is known by scientists today.

One study involved Kirlian's photographs of leaves. As the leaves withered, the photos showed their auras (bio-energy fields) withered as well. This knowledge was used to detect stress in athletes to help them to increase their performance levels.

As a consequence of this research, Dr David Hawkins, a psychiatrist and consciousness researcher, went on to prove that all objects as well as people have energy, and that all atoms and sub-atoms are nothing more than energy. Furthermore, this energy vibrates on the scale of consciousness.

He summed up his research in his groundbreaking book *Power vs Force*.[8] He was able to identify and create a scale of consciousness where, depending on your vibrational frequency, your emotional health and happiness determined your physical outcome and lifestyle, discovering that your energy doesn't just affect life, it affects those around you, too. Either by lifting your vibrational levels or lowering them, you create either love and happiness or anxiety and stress.

---

8   D Hawkins, *Power vs Force: An anatomy of consciousness* (Veritas, 2012)

The Hawkins Scale of Consciousness has a total of seventeen levels that go in ascending order: shame, guilt, apathy, grief, fear, desire, anger, pride, courage, neutrality, willingness, acceptance, reason, love, joy, peace and enlightenment.[9]

In an article discussing levels of consciousness, Steve Pavlina believes that people move between levels, but the majority of the population would be between courage and reason, with very few people reaching the higher levels within their lifetimes.[10]

You can check out YouTube for clips of Hawkins talking about the scale and how to reach advanced states of consciousness.[11]

The most powerful of emotions

The strongest of all emotions is love. It radiates at the highest energetic frequency, according to the HeartMath Institute.[12]

Accepting that everything is energy has helped me to understand how Jack, now free of his physical body, is able to be in communication with me. When my energy

---

9   More information and purchase of the scale can be found at Veritas Publishing, https://veritaspub.com/map-of-consciousness/

10 S Pavlina, 'Levels Of Consciousness – David R. Hawkins', Awaken (2018), https://awaken.com/2018/07/levels-of-consciousness

11 DR Hawkins, *Advanced States of Consciousness, Volume 3* (Veritas Publishing, 2003), www.youtube.com/watch?v=G_eK-R9EDOk

12 S Childre, 'Raising our vibration through compassion and unconditional love' (blog post, 4 April 2017), www.heartmath.org

frequency levels are high, experiencing emotions of joy and love, I transcend emotions of grief and sadness. Combine this with my own psychic/spiritual abilities and Jack's love, in addition to our connection to the divine universal power of love, our 'communication' through the veil becomes clearer and stronger. Love never dies. Souls are timeless, boundless, outside of time.

Therapeutic energy techniques

As a practitioner, I have found all these complementary therapies helpful, both for myself and for helping other people experiencing grief and loss.

- Reiki can assist you in feeling more peaceful, calm and relaxed, boosting your natural energy system and raising your vibrational level.

- Hypnotherapy is a great technique to relax you and help address any negative thoughts and behaviours.

- HypnoReiki™ is a combination of reiki and hypnotherapy which I developed in 2016.

- EFT, also known as tapping, is great to release immediate emotional distress and anxiety, an extremely valuable self-help tool. EFT (Emotional Freedom Technique) is a meridian energy therapy. Just like acupuncture it works directly on the meridian system of the body, but instead of needles the major meridian points are stimulated by tapping on them lightly. It combines the physical effects of the meridian treatment with the mental effects of focusing on the emotional distress of the problem which evokes release and relief. It was designed and developed by Gary Craig from Dr Roger Callahan's Thought Field Therapy (TFT).

- It is a simple yet effective self-help technique designed for ease of use so that everyone can benefit without prior knowledge of meridians. All ages can use it to help reduce stress and tension, and a full range of emotional, mental, spiritual and even physical difficulties.

- The EFT tapping points are situated on the face, collarbone, underarm and hands. A qualified practitioner will help show you where they are and how to do it for yourself.

It is important to reiterate here that grief cannot be cured as such. These energy techniques work well when used holistically alongside grief counselling. They will bring you comfort – physically, mentally, emotionally and spiritually – and energetic nourishment.

Energy centres

There are many chakras in the body, but in reiki we tend to work with seven main ones. Although not seen with the naked eye, the chakras contain your energetic body's connective fields. These points are central connectors which can get clogged up like a house gutter does with leaves and debris, so new energy cannot flow freely around your body. These blockages need to be removed and the energetic body lines cleared, balanced, harmonised to allow fresh new energy into your body for your optimum health and wellbeing, physically, mentally, emotionally and spiritually.

For more information on the chakras, you may like to read my blog.[13]

You may also be interested to read my own personal journey with reiki.[14]

Scientific research

Although reiki is an ancient healing technique, there is scientific research today that backs up its merits. Dr Ann Baldwin, PhD has researched it extensively and recently written a science-based book on the subject supporting the benefits of reiki.[15] Many hospitals in the United States now provide regular reiki treatments as

---

13   J Sackett Wood, 'A Guide to the Reiki Chakras' (blog post, 6 February 2019), www.hypnoreiki.co.uk/a-guide-to-the-reiki-chakras
14   J Sackett Wood, 'Becoming a Reiki Master Teacher – Joy's journey' (blog post, 13 January 2019), www.hypnoreiki.co.uk/becoming-a-reiki-master-teacher-joys-journey
15   A Baldwin, *Reiki in Clinical Practice: A science-based guide* (Handspring Publishing, 2020)

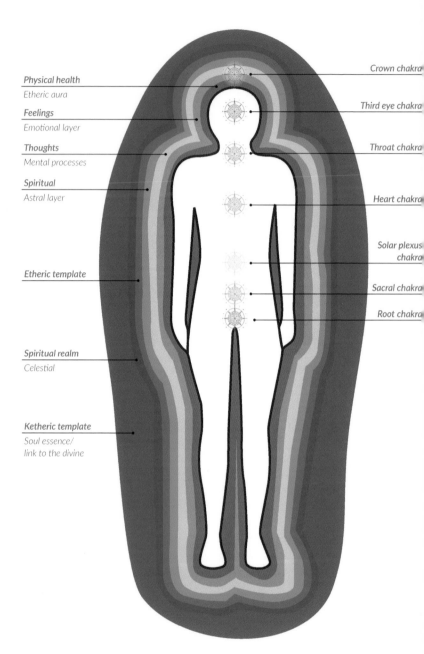

Physical health
Etheric aura

Feelings
Emotional layer

Thoughts
Mental processes

Spiritual
Astral layer

Etheric template

Spiritual realm
Celestial

Ketheric template
Soul essence/
link to the divine

Crown chakra

Third eye chakra

Throat chakra

Heart chakra

Solar plexus
chakra

Sacral chakra

Root chakra

The chakras and aura/bio-energy fields

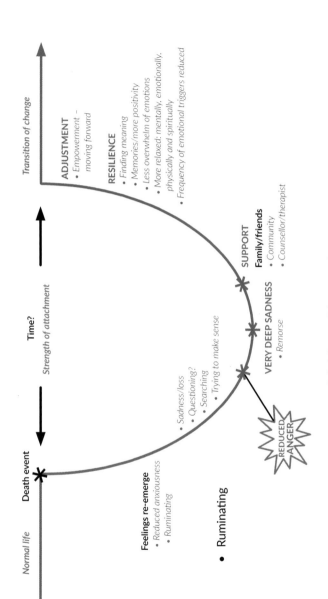

Normal life   Death event

Transition of change

Time?

Strength of attachment

Feelings re-emerge
- *Reduced anxiousness*
- *Ruminating*

- *Sadness/loss*
- *Questioning?*
- *Searching*
- *Trying to make sense*

VERY DEEP SADNESS
- *Remorse*

SUPPORT
Family/friends
- *Community*
- *Counsellor/therapist*

REDUCED ANGER

- Ruminating

ADJUSTMENT
- *Empowerment – moving forward*

RESILIENCE
- *Finding meaning*
- *Memories/more positivity*
- *Less overwhelm of emotions*
- *More relaxed: mentally, emotionally, physically and spiritually*
- *Frequency of emotional triggers reduced*

Grief Curve, Diagram 1C

taste and touch. Therefore, intuition is accepted as an aspect of our spirituality.

What is spirituality?

'The spiritual life is part of the human essence. It is a defining characteristic of human nature, without which human nature is not fully human.'[16]
— Abraham Maslow

Spirituality is an integral part of being human. Psychologist Abraham Maslow developed a hierarchy of human needs, of which spirituality/transcendence is the highest of all. The following diagram is based on Maslow's Hierarchy of Needs.

---

16   J Bradshaw, *Healing the Shame that Binds You* (USA: Health and Communications, Revised Edition, 2005)

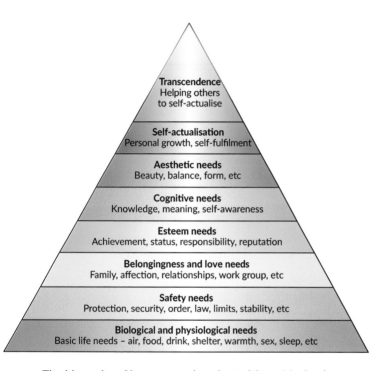

The hierarchy of human needs, adapted from Maslow's Hierarchy of Needs (Maslow, AH, 'A theory of human motivation', Psychological Review, 50/4 (1943), 370-396, https://doi.org/10.1037/h0054346)

Some people connect spirituality with religion, but it doesn't have to be. Spirituality is to do with your inner life; it is about love, truth, goodness, giving and caring. It is about values and meaning, our innate sense of awe and wonder at the mysteries of life. To many, spirituality is about wholeness and completion, our ultimate human need.

The nature of spirituality causes us to transcend ourselves to connect with an ultimate source of reality. The death of a loved one almost forces us to connect with the spiritual aspect of ourselves. A large part of the grief process is questioning, trying to make sense of what has happened to our loved one, and what will eventually happen to us (see Grief Curve, Diagram 1B). Death makes us question life:

- What is it all about?

- Why am I here?

- Where has my loved one gone?

- What is death?

- What is the meaning and purpose of this life?

- Why has this happened to my loved one?

- Why has this happened to me?

- Where will I go when I die?

- Will my loved one be waiting for me?

These are among the many questions that leave us seeking answers. This is normal – the loss of our loved one has had a significant impact on our life and has changed it in many ways. The psychological adapting period we experience creates a space to review our life and reassess our values and what really matters most to us.

It is not unusual to find ourselves wondering why we have continued in some aspects of our life that haven't made us happy. If we have been hanging on to areas of our life that no longer serve us, we may make the decision at this time to let these go.

The death of a loved one also makes us question our sense of God and the afterlife. For some, it can challenge their faith.

CASE STUDY: HELEN

Helen had grown up and remained a devout Catholic. Within the space of just six years, she experienced the death of her niece, her great niece, her mother and uncle. The impact of these traumatic losses seriously affected her faith and relationship with God. The deep sadness she felt turned into depression and a sleep disorder.

I helped Helen in a variety of ways, firstly by giving her the ability to take back power for herself in what seemed a powerless situation by teaching her some relaxation tools and techniques. She initially came for HypnoReiki™, which proved very successful for her. Then she worked through her feelings regarding each death.

Through having the opportunity to voice her feelings about God openly and without judgement, she came to forgive God for taking her beloved ones from her, believing they were now happy in Heaven. Helen felt able to move on in life herself, slept better and enjoyed a better relationship with her husband because of it.

For others, faith can bring comfort.

CASE STUDY: ROSA

Rosa believed she was able to cope with the grief and death of her adored brother because, in her own words, 'I have a strong Christian belief and know that one day, I will see him again – he will be fit and able to walk. I often dream of the great hug he will give me when I pass through the veil and see him with our parents.'

The bigger picture of faith and belief

In my understanding, spirituality, religion, psychology, philosophy, sociology, anthropology are all entwined, inter-related. During my theological and philosophical studies, I was most interested to learn that there has never been one community or civilisation that anthropologists and archaeologists have known to exist, no matter how isolated, that has not had a sense of the sacred and an afterlife. Evidence from ancient burial sites of religious artefacts, cave drawings and paintings, etc back up the expression of spirituality as part of human nature, and formalised religion as the outward physical expression of spirituality. After thousands of years of human existence, I think that is quite impressive and convincing.

I learnt that all the world's religions are based on the organisation of beliefs, teachings and rituals within the framework of the history and culture of particular spiritual founders and leaders. Spirituality is the essence of all religions and all the religions share the same spiritual qualities of love, truth, goodness, giving, caring and love of God – The Divine. Spirituality is within your human essence and outside of you in the ultimate higher essence of God, or whatever name you are comfortable with and understand God to be.

Philosophy and life after death

A large part of grief is thinking about the 'big questions', as they are known in philosophy. In fact, these questions are the very basis of philosophy. The word philosophy means the study of wisdom. From the ancient Greek philosophers to the present day, the discussions and debates continue regarding the meaning of life, morals and ethics, why we are here, the existence of God, humankind and spirituality, etc. As a consequence, we are all philosophers.

From a young age, I have had a belief in something greater than myself and the existence of an afterlife. When I reflect, I can map my spiritual journey throughout my life. I am wondering if you can too. Perhaps you would like to journal your thoughts – I would love to hear them. If you are happy to share them, please email them to me at joy@joysackettwood.com.

Religion, culture and identity

If you were born and raised in India, it is likely you will be a Hindu. If you were born and raised in the Middle East, you are probably a Muslim. If you were born and raised in Italy, I would guess you are a Christian Catholic.

In England, we are of the Christian culture inasmuch as we follow Christian holidays (Easter, Christmas, etc), although only 11% of the population actually attends church regularly now. But in my experience, most people, unless they are confirmed believers of another faith, would say they are Christian and put Church of England down on application forms in answer to 'What is your religious identity?' You may say you are agnostic, which means you don't know and are still making your mind up whether or not to follow a particular religion, or an atheist who has no belief in a god or spirituality. You may say you are humanist – that is, you believe in the good spirit of humankind – or you may say you are spiritual in that you believe in something, but you don't know what.

If you went to school in England or an English school abroad, you will probably have had Christian values and beliefs taught to you, whether it was a church school or not, because Christianity is the very fibre of English society. The heart of our social and moral structure lies within the teachings of Christianity, as do the principles of our education, law, court and penal systems, based on reward and punishment. Whatever your religious and cultural identity and beliefs, they will have been shaped by your upbringing and education.

PERSONAL EXPERIENCE

In the months leading up to when Jack died, he had become extremely reflective, spiritual and philosophical. We enjoyed many stimulating conversations together. I believe he had a spiritual awakening and enlightenment experience. I also believe, due to this, that his soul had evolved. Some spiritualists say Jack had fulfilled his purpose in his earthly lifetime.

During my times of being introspective, I have come to understand how much I have learnt and evolved, personally and spiritually, from being Jack's mum. I have come to believe this is the meaning and purpose of both our lives.

> Every cloud has a silver lining. Death makes us think about life, and working through these reflections promotes the transformational power of grief and loss.

Faith is to have a belief, a knowingness in the unseen, the non-physical. This is the metaphysical.

When I ask people if they have any particular religious beliefs, it is to help me to understand them and respect their identity. The majority say something like, 'Well, I do believe in something, but I don't know what.' Then they will usually go on to say that yes, they are spiritual.

What people often say is that they are put off by religious fundamentalism. They also say religion has, in the main, lost contact with the majority of people. No matter how funkily a modern church may market itself, they think religious leaders are unable to connect with the people of today due to the religion's teachings being rooted in ancient history and culture. On the other hand, 'spirituality' encompasses a wider and more relevant conscious appeal.

Comfort in the established faiths

Traditional religion can offer comfort and solace in times of grief. Places of worship such as churches, with services, music, songs and rituals that have remained the same for years, can bring a sense of security in an insecure episode of your life.

In Western culture, most funerals are held within a church or crematorium with familiar prayers, hymns and rituals. Although services are more flexible these days to accommodate the changes in society, a lot of people still like to feel connected to their history and ancestors. It brings a sense of belonging, being part of a community. In this way, grieving people may find the answers to their questions.

Life needs meaning

CASE STUDY: ROB

Working with people suffering from long-term depression, I have learnt the root cause of low mood and apathy towards life is generally having no sense of direction, meaning or purpose. And as a consequence, a lack of spiritual connection.

Rob, a young male client, didn't see the point of living because in the end, as he said, 'We die anyway.' Exploring his thinking in relation to his early life, we discovered he had survived a serious car crash at the age of eight when he spent a week in a coma with head injuries and several weeks in hospital. His PTSD had never been acknowledged; he still suffered flashbacks and symptoms associated with the trauma twenty years later.

Through counselling, he found a liking for philosophy and ethics, and went on to study them. Consequently, he enjoyed a new outlook on life, and death, and came to be happier and healthier with a sense of wellbeing.

Rob just needed to voice his experiences in a safe, non-judgemental environment, explore his thoughts and find his direction in life. Healthy thinking and questioning are the route to wisdom, according to the philosophers.

When you're engaging in your rational self, the mind that reasons, the analytical left brain is activated. Allowing your intuition and instincts to engage, you are connecting with your creative, imaginative, spiritual right brain, searching and experiencing beyond cognitive logic and bridging the gap between the conscious and non-conscious parts of the mind, between instinct and reason. Keeping an open mind without fear or judgement is an emotionally and socially mature activity. Simply allow your intuition to guide you to seek to understand and make sense of your grief experience.

Using intuition successfully in business

Some people worry about following their intuition in business. They wonder if they may be judged, or even judge themselves for not fully using the logical part of their brain in making decisions. Western culture has undermined the intuitive aspect of our humanity, but just think how many people have succeeded in business by following their instincts, their intuition and their logical thinking all at once.

For good examples of this, I suggest you watch the television series *Dragons' Den* or *The Apprentice* and observe the panel of entrepreneurs, like Lord Alan Sugar, Deborah Meaden, Peter Jones, Touker Suleyman. See how they use their business knowledge and intuition to decide which contestants they are prepared to invest their money in. Observe their body language and how they are weighing up the body language of the contestant, looking into the eyes of the contestant. What the entrepreneurs are doing is using their innate ability to tune into the contestants as they pitch and defend their business ideas, intuitively connecting with the essence of the contestants to make their judgements. By doing this, the entrepreneurs are engaging on a deep energetic level with the contestant.

If you read the biographies of many great creatives and visionaries, historical entrepreneurs and successful leaders in business, they will tell similar stories of how they were inspired to start their business offering a particular product or service, and by holding on to their intuition and vision, believing in their offering's value to others, they ensured their business plans eventually came into being. While others may have mocked them, they held on to their convictions to prove the naysayers wrong. Great examples are Henry Ford, Dame Anita Roddick, Sir Richard Branson and Sir James Dyson, to name but a few.

Science, religion and spirituality

When Galileo proved the earth is round, not flat as had been believed for centuries at the time, he expressed this as a truth. And as a consequence, he was persecuted by everyone, from his own scientific colleagues to the traditional religious leaders. Why? Galileo had produced evidence that seriously challenged the entrenched religious beliefs of his day.

This was also the case with Charles Darwin, whose origin of the species theory totally upset the established beliefs and teachings in the holy books of many religions. And the Creationist belief verses the Scientific Evolutionist theory remains an issue today among fundamentalist Christians, especially in the United States, dividing communities and politics.

Theology and spirituality

A lot of people still think science and theology contradict each other. Theology means the study of all things connected to God, 'Theo' being the Greek word for God and 'ology' meaning the study of. In my studies thirty-five years ago, I was excited to discover that many Christian theologians are scientists who have developed a harmonious understanding of the universe using methods and discoveries of modern science. This is well explained by John Polkinghorne KBE FRS, a former Cambridge professor of mathematical physics, in his book *One World*.[17] In recent years, Einstein's theory of relativity and quantum physics has helped to explain universal laws, multi-levels of consciousness, the spiritual and spirituality, and humans as multi-dimensional beings.

When you're seeking to make sense of grief and life experiences, it is helpful to know about this. Why? Because you, like a lot of people whose loved one has died, are likely to ask the question 'Where has my loved one gone?' or 'Who or what is God?' or 'Why has God done this to me?' Many people coming to me for grief counselling have told me that they have seriously wondered about the rationality of God and why God, who is supposed to be all good and all loving, allows such pain and suffering to happen to them personally and in the world, and 'Why do good people die young and bad people live a long life?' These are questions which the philosophers and theologians since the days of Ancient Greece have all attempted to explain.

To explore these big questions is a human activity. It feeds the part of us that taps in to mysteries like a

---

17   JC Polkinghorne, *One World: The interaction of science and theology* (Templeton Foundation Press, 2007)

curious child embarking on a great adventure, or it can be filled with angst. It depends on our own personal experiences, intuition and subjectivity. This is why faith in God, however you understand God, has always been one of the most difficult things to argue, prove, express and explain.

What is faith?

Faith is believing in something that's unseen and intangible, taking us away from the human world into a mysterious unknown world of the immaterial. Some people find this fascinating, other people find it frightening. Evidence of a God figure is based on personal experience, which is hard to prove.

Some say the actions of a person who has faith in God is proof enough, evidence of the existence of God whose nature is reflected in the believer's personality and character. But this could lead to a lot more questions as we humans are essentially imperfect, and God is said to be perfection. Perfection is too much to live up to, so many believers experience low self-esteem and self-worth when they get caught up in the high expectations of religious belief.

On the other hand, a commitment to religious faith can give a person structure and security in their lives, as well as a sense of belonging, social companionship and community. In my professional experiences with people who have a confirmed faith and strong belief, they are more able to become resilient and cope with grief better than those who do not.

This is confirmed by my husband and business partner in Swans Therapy, John:

CASE STUDY: JOHN

'I have worked as a volunteer bereavement counsellor for a local palliative cancer care unit for almost twelve years and gained much experience, not only from initial and ongoing training, but also from seeing many clients over that time.

'The question of faith almost always arises at some time during the grief process and can be a tricky subject to deal with as it is wholly dependent on the client's beliefs within the many cultural differences we share today. When someone is in such a vulnerable state of mind, a strong faith, whichever faith that may be, can be a great source of strength and comfort, but equally that faith can be severely challenged and many questions raised by the death of a loved one: "Why did God let this happen?" "What have I done to deserve this?" "Why am I being punished so harshly?" "Why has He abandoned me?"

'Any response to these questions is difficult. While I have my own faith, I accept that it may not concur with other people's in all aspects. General words of comfort are never enough, but challenging people's faith is a slippery path to travel. I have found that most people with faith will come back to it in their own time. Then, and only then, will it truly bring them comfort.

'There are, of course, those without faith. I recall one particular client who told me several times that he believed in nothing at all. When you die, that's the end of it.

'As our sessions went on, I felt compelled to ask him, when he thought about his wife, where he imagined her to be. His answer was simple. Although he still loved her dearly and missed her every day, he didn't have to worry about where she was as he believed she wasn't anywhere. I would add here that this client needed grief support for over a year, two to three times longer than most clients I have worked with.'

Ways to develop your intuition

Learning to meditate will deepen your understanding of the spiritual and sense of the sacred. Although listening to your intuition and acting on it takes a bit of practice, once you become attuned to it, you will wonder how you managed when you were less aware of it.

Intuition is a part of you that will bring a deeper sense of peace and connection to yourself, the wider world and beyond. This is yours and yours alone, your authentic self, the you that is unique and special. It is a fact that there is absolutely no other person like you in the whole of existence, which makes you a miracle and a part of the Divine. As you learn to open up and trust this aspect of yourself, you fill in the gaps to experience satisfying fulfilment, integrating your emotional and social intelligence with the sense of the sacred becoming consciously aware that you are a multi-dimensional being.

To progress on this, it will be helpful to learn to align the six aspects of yourself:

1. Your thinking self – head

2. Your feeling self – heart

3. Your intuition – gut feeling

4. Your inspirational self – senses

5. Your spiritual self – higher consciousness

6. Your evolutionary self – soul

Of course, the loss of your loved one may feel like the worst thing that could ever have happened to you. Engaging in these activities as a daily routine will help you to develop your intuition. At the same time, they will enable you to find the answers to the big questions for yourself, shift your perceptions, build your resilience and move you nearer to coming to terms with the death of your loved one:

- Meditate – ten to twenty minutes will help you to learn not to think so much and wonder more.

- Gratitude – a good habit to get into. Say thank you for the good and positive things in your life as this will raise your energy frequencies and lift your spirits.

- Visualise – promote imagination.

- Engage in creativity of any gentle kind.

- Writing and journalling – express your thoughts through words.

- Prayer and contemplation – seek and send loving support for yourself and others.

- Live from the heart – love, care and feel compassion for yourself and others.

- Affirmations – practise positive self-talk, always starting statements with 'I am…'

Suggestions to help you

- Understand that wondering about the meaning of life and death, and other big questions, is normal and healthy during grief.

- Learn what intuition and spirituality are, and how they can help you in your grief.

- Understand that faith can help or hinder you, depending on your point of view right now. Don't feel guilty about this as true believers always come back to their faith eventually.

- See that science and theology are connected, not in conflict.

- Recognise the importance of using intuition in business.

- Practise meditation and other techniques to build your resilience.

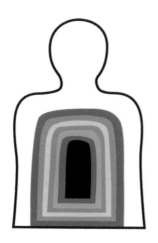

SEVEN

Building The Seventh Layer Of RESILIENCE

Empowerment – confidence, strength, new learnings, knowledge, expansion (personal growth).

As you move through the Grief Curve, Diagram 1C and build the layers of resilience, you may find that the frequency of emotional triggers relating to your loved one starts to reduce. Hopefully you are no longer feeling so fragile and vulnerable as the intensity of your emotions become less overwhelming, your brain having had the chance to establish a new pattern of thinking in experiencing life without your loved one. By engaging in the activities and suggestions I've shared so far in this book, you will have helped yourself to speed up the process of transition.

In this chapter, you will see how your inner strength and resolve will help you to make changes, adapt to your loss, and build positive confidence in yourself that will give you a new lease of life and empower you. You will continue to learn about my own personal journey with grief and read examples of how I managed loss and change. Then I will explain how I came to be able to connect with my son in spirit and enjoy a new relationship with him, helping you to learn how you can connect with your own loved one, offering you suggestions to explore this for yourself if you feel inclined to do so.

Grief can make us change in a positive way

CASE STUDY: SUE

In the early stage of her grief after the death of her husband, Sue struggled with making decisions and being assertive. As time went by, she really had to start making important decisions for herself that affected her and her two children.

As her husband had not been a practical man, she began by making repairs and renovations to their home. When she saw the benefits and results of this work, Sue really began to enjoy her new creativity. She had found skills and abilities within herself, and other aspects of herself she didn't know she had.

Sue also made decisions on enjoyable family activities. Although on one level she was still grieving for her husband, through her new experiences, Sue found that her confidence and self-esteem noticeably increased over an eighteen-month period, and she enjoyed the empowerment this gave her. On this level, she felt so much stronger, more capable, independent and in control of her life.

Death can bring positive changes

For some, the death of a loved one may come as a relief, especially if they have been physically or mentally ill for a long time and death brings a form of release from their pain and suffering. If you have been a long-term carer for a loved one, you may now be feeling able to do the things you have been wanting to do, but haven't been able to do for a while due to the lack of time and your commitments. If this is the case, engage in those activities – go out to places, visit friends, travel, take a holiday unrestricted by the responsibility of caring for your loved one.

For many of us, visiting residential care homes, checking in with a loved one's practical needs, can dominate our lives. When the care of a loved one has been demanding on us physically, mentally and emotionally, finding ourselves free from the routine can give us a new lease of life.

There is nothing to feel guilty or ashamed about. Your loved one would have wanted you to carry on with your life and have fun. Many people I have spoken to who have experienced this have said that when they've allowed themselves to live life to the full again, they have felt re-energised. The surge of renewed energy enables them to adapt to a new way of life in a positive way.

Some people have told me they'd stayed in unhappy relationships, work environments or situations prior to the death of their loved one, and that the death actually motivated them to decide what they did and didn't want in their lives. They often say things like, 'It made me realise life is too short to continue to waste my time and efforts on unhappy, unrewarding situations and relationships.' Forced to face the finality of life, they took the opportunity and were motivated to make important, empowering changes.

PERSONAL EXPERIENCE

Following the deaths of my brother and father just two months apart in 2005, I decided to move away from teaching after twenty years to set up my own business. Before they'd died, I had already made a conscious decision not to stay in teaching into my elder years, so I felt strong in making this decision, the right one for me.

Teaching was my second career. I wanted to blend my skills and knowledge as a fashion designer/ tailoress with my passion for the Fairtrade movement into an ethical business that expressed my values. I opened a shop in which I produced a collection of designer clothes using Fairtrade fabrics from overseas, and a range of fashion accessories and jewellery from various women's projects worldwide.

As a visionary, I focused my philosophy on an ethical business based on Fairtrade principles. The mainly male-dominated business groups I attended at the time didn't understand this. As far as I was aware, there were no support groups expressly for businesswomen at that time.

Despite the incredible support of my husband and friends, this business, which ran for six years, was a steep learning curve. I had to learn all aspects of business the hard way, and quickly. As well as organising and attending events, trade shows and craft fairs, designing and making clothes and running the shop, I also gave sewing lessons. Those experiences served me well when I transferred six years of knowledge into my counselling and psychotherapy business, Swans Therapy.

My husband has always been my business partner. When we launched Swans Therapy in 2008, initially as hypnotherapists, we trained together and qualified together, adding several other therapeutic modalities and treatments since then. We make a good team as we share an understanding of the therapeutic business and its needs and demands. As a couple, we have been together since 2003, so he has been there for me through all my personal grief experiences, too, and has been an incredible support.

Having the support of family and friends is really important because they will be directly affected by the decisions you make.

Change as another form of grief and loss

If clients say to me they want to change their careers or start their own business when they are going through the process of grief, I am able to support them appropriately due to experiences I have had personally. I would always suggest they err on the side of caution. A slow and planned transition makes the journey smoother.

What is important if you're planning a major change in your life is to do a lot of research, talk to experts about your idea, listen with an open mind to solid business and financial advice, get a circle of people around you to support you and make sure you choose a good time to launch yourself into the change.

PERSONAL EXPERIENCE

Leaving teaching, I now understand, triggered a form of grief in me as I adapted to the change in my lifestyle and identity. I wish I had known about the process of grief then as it would have better prepared me for the changes, such as the loss of status and a secure income I'd had from being committed to my teaching profession, which is why I include it in this book. My identity as a teacher over a twenty-year journey to reach the position I had achieved had taken a lot of hard work and dedication. I didn't know enough about how the grief and loss related to this massive change in my life would affect me.

I mourned the loss of the relationship I'd had with my teaching profession on so many levels: my teaching friends, my colleagues, my students, the subjects I taught. I had no idea how removing myself from these relationships would impact on me, even though it was what I wanted. I absolutely knew I had outgrown teaching as a full-time career when I stopped loving the work due to the overwhelming influence of school politics, educational structures, unrealistic demands and expectations, inspections. All these served to strangle my passion for teaching, and I didn't want these stresses and strains to impact my professionalism or my health, but my love of teaching my subject and educating young people has never waned. Neither has my love for learning. All learning, academically and in life, mentally, emotionally and spiritually, is essential for our personal expansion and growth.

It took a while for me to adapt as I didn't expect the consequences of my choice of timing. I had unconsciously added to my grief for my brother and father in making such a big change at that particular time, so I found going through this transition challenging on various levels.

It may sound contradictory, but I literally had to wean myself away from teaching through taking on short contracts and some supply work while running my business and training to be a professional counsellor. I was not aware that moving away from teaching constituted another big loss, even though it was of my own choice.

Empowering yourself and others

As I have learnt, all experiences are learning experiences, the good as well as the not so good. Everything has a higher purpose, even grief and the loss of a loved one to death. When we raise our consciousness in the search for meaning and purpose, at the same time choosing not to suffer in our loss, we are raising our energy vibrations to feel confident and empowered.

People do this in many ways. They may decide to raise money and support a charity, for example Cancer Relief if cancer was the cause of their loved one's death.

They may decide to start a charity to address an issue connected to their loved one. They may set up a trust in their loved one's memory or name.

Being able to make sense of and see a purpose in your loss and putting that purpose into action, doing something positive as a result of your sadness, is so uplifting. You may even discover something completely new and exciting as a direct result of your grieving process.

Empowering business support groups

In more recent years, I have attended various local business support groups. For the past three years, I have been a member of Western Women Mean Business (WWMB). This is not a networking group as such, but we do support each other's businesses wherever we can.

When I experienced the death of my son, I felt extremely supported by WWMB's values of learn, grow and contribute. Being part of this group gives me focus, a sense of belonging, friendship, security and acceptance. As members, we are evolving together as we are challenged to expand our consciousness to become all that we can be as the multi-dimensional beings we are. I find this an extremely empowering and energetically uplifting experience.

Empowering your mind

We are continuingly self-transforming, and grief can take us on a new and exciting transformational journey.

Author Joe Dispenza in his books *You Are the Placebo* and *Becoming Supernatural* and in a YouTube video interview with Tom Bilyeu, says that when we choose to change our mindset, we move from victim to creator.[18, 19] He explains our unconscious analytical mind is wired up to keep us safe in survival mode, and 70% of most humans' life is existing subconsciously in this state of mind. Our previous life experiences of trauma and difficult events, and our emotional attachments to them, remain stuck in our thought patterns. They then imprint into the cells of our physical bodies. This means we are always on high alert, producing stress hormones that cause the disease in our bodies.

We all feel fear, anger, aggression, suffering, shame, jealousy, etc, but scientific evidence shows that when we engage in meditation, it slows down the brainwaves and enables us to practise silencing the analytical mind to promote positive emotions, inner peace and joy.[20]

---

18   J Dispenza, *You Are the Placebo: Making your mind matter* (Hay House, 2014) and *Becoming Supernatural: How common people are doing the uncommon* (Hay House, 2017)

19   J Dispenza, 'How to Unlock the Full Potential of Your Mind' (June 2018), www.youtube.com/watch?v=La9oLLoI5Rc

20   AG Walton, '7 ways meditation can actually change the brain', *Forbes* (2015), www.forbes.com/sites/alicegwalton/2015/02/09/7-ways-meditation-can-actually-change-the-brain

These all help to boost the physical body's immune system as each and every cell is positively changed. As a consequence, we move from living unconsciously to living consciously.

Knowledge is power and knowledge of self is self-empowerment.[21] External factors do not make people happy. Empowered people have less need for material things to be happy; they feel the happiness from within, which comes from a sense of knowing that they have individual power and the ability to empower and recreate themselves.

Our thoughts and emotions are energy. We are multi-dimensional energy beings, mentally, emotionally, spiritually and energetically interconnected. I really came to know and understand this through the death of my son, Jack.

Power within curiosity and the unexpected

The most empowering experience I have had since the death of my son is discovering that our relationship continues, just in a different way. I've learnt love literally survives death. Love never dies. Another

---

21   J Dispenza, 'How to Unlock the Full Potential of Your Mind' (June 2018), www.youtube.com/watch?v=La9oLLoI5Rc

existence without the physical body goes on beyond the veil, and it is all about energy and the power of love.

As I explained in Chapter Five, the emotion of love vibrates to the highest energy frequency. As a rational thinker, I have always sought to find evidence for super-rational experiences and have learnt that the science of quantum physics backs up how love keeps the essence of us, our soul and spirit, connected to our loved ones, even after death. This is how our loved ones are able to remain connected to us.

In addition to building our spiritual power, we can enhance our receptivity to our loved ones. The 'veil' is simply our physical body, which vibrates at a lower, heavier frequency than our energetic and spiritual body. We can all learn to switch on this connection should we choose to do so, and switch it off. I will return to this in more detail later in the book.

To satisfy my curiosity and as part of my own personal development, I attended an excellent evidential spiritual mediumship course taught by an exceptionally gifted, intelligent, grounded woman called Suzanne Giesemann. I had realised for a while I was open to being psychic, claircognisant, having a sense of clear knowing, as I could feel the presence of higher powers helping me in my counselling work. The timing for me was perfect; I learnt so much from this course, which I will share in more detail later.

PERSONAL EXPERIENCE

Jack's ability to communicate with me from beyond the veil started immediately and spontaneously from the time I heard about his death. I had in a way been developing psychically and spiritually over a period of a few years since attending a development group run by my reiki teacher. I was sceptical at first, but kept an open mind.

My journey had been slow, but steady. I'd had some messages from my brother and father, who died in 2005, and my mother who died in 2011. These were mainly personal, given to me directly or through mediums I had seen on the odd occasion. I was interested, but not especially involved. At times, I would receive a message for a friend from their loved one who had passed over, which seemed to help them, but nothing on a regular basis.

The general idea of mediumship came naturally to me as I work with couples in relationship counselling and coaching, often in the role of mediator, relying on intuition and instinct. As I continued my journey with reiki, progressing through the different levels, I became more sensitive to the flow of energy and healing. My claircognisance – clear knowing using extra-sensory feelings – and clairvoyance – clear seeing using extra-sensory vision – developed with my being able to see symbols and images in my mind's eye which helped to deepen the treatments and healing. As these came so naturally and instinctively to me, I made the decision to attend spiritual development workshops, just out of curiosity, when I had the time to do so.

Add to this the fact that my son and I always did have an uncanny telepathic connection when he was here in physical form, especially in the year leading up to his death, and we had talked at great length philosophically and spiritually. I believe my son had a spiritual awakening experience before he transitioned to the spirit realm.

Although the news of Jack's death shook me to the core, I felt a strong sense of his presence. While telling his sister the bad news face to face was heartbreaking emotionally, I also felt a sharp physical pain in my right leg and instantly knew this was part of the cause of his death. I found out later he'd had a blood clot in his right thigh.

Throughout the funeral arrangements, I felt him guiding and helping me to make difficult decisions on his behalf. I knew he wouldn't want anything too traditional and I wanted to do something unique for him, so I got a strong urge to paint a symbolically meaningful design on the lid of his coffin. I used to make hand-painted birthday cards for him as a child, and it seemed this was something he would like me to do as an act of love to celebrate his new spirit birthday.

I meditated and, going with a design that came into my mind's eye, I painted a rainbow in a blue sky with white clouds, hearts in the rainbow chakra colours and floating white feathers. Below the brass plate with his name on it, I painted a large red heart. I had intended to place my favourite photo of him in the middle of it as a tribute, but that night, my sleep was restless. The finished coffin lid was being picked up at 9am by the funeral directors, but something was not right.

I got a feeling that Jack didn't like the red heart. It was such a strong feeling that I got up in the early hours and painted over the red heart with white paint. Then a sense of peace came over me and it just felt right.

During the funeral ceremony, a lifelong friend read a tribute she'd written to Jack. In it, she mentioned how red hearts are associated with this life, the physical temporal world we live in and romantic love, while white hearts represent purity and spirituality, the spiritual world, the completeness of peace, the eternal presence of love. You could have knocked me down with a feather! A red heart would certainly not have been appropriate from a mother to her son on his coffin. Our new spiritual connection and relationship had begun.

I made a video of the artwork I did if you would like to see it on my Facebook page: www.facebook.com/Joysackettwood

Since the two-hour 'swingy thing' conversation I had with Jack that I told you about in Chapter Four, I have been in no doubt that I've been talking to my son. We have regular conversations now which excite me and bring me much comfort. He still has a great sense of humour and loves to make me laugh and keep me cheerful, and a lot of what he tells me that I didn't previously know can be verified. Of course, I miss him in the physical world, but since I have been able to talk to him beyond the veil, our relationship has gone from strength to strength. Jack is a different soul now he is in spirit; he helps me with my work and healing.

I know it was Jack who directed me to enrol on a course to learn about evidential mediumship.

What is evidential mediumship?

Evidential mediumship is when a spiritual medium provides clear facts related to a person's loved one and proves their continued existence in spirit, either through an individual reading or a group demonstration. Being newly drawn to this fascinating subject and feeling the desire to learn more, I have been amazed to discover how well my son is able to communicate with me and help me in so many ways. I am proud of his newfound skills and abilities in spirit. Our ongoing relationship has given me a surge of energy and zest for life. I am learning, growing and expanding so much about and around this subject. My son is teaching me and I feel truly good, happy and empowered by this.

Empowerment comes hand in hand with confidence, and confidence comes from reassurance. You can accelerate your adapting, moving through the transition in your life without your loved one, by finding a way to honour them. This book is mine.

I have discovered that living a happy, fulfilled life, packed with love, shifts our spiritual self from contraction to expansion. This is the way that our loved ones would want us to live our lives: fully and happily, until we meet again.

Suggestions to help you

- Understand and take strength from the fact that grief can change you in a positive way.

- Change can bring about its own form of grief. If you are making life-changing decisions while going through the process of grief, make sure you empower yourself with support and listen to good advice.

- Choose not to suffer in your loss, instead raising your energy vibrations to feel confident and empowered.

- Allow yourself to have an open mind to new discoveries. There's power within the unexpected.

- Consider what you have learnt positively from your loved one's death.

- Consider having a one-to-one reading with a reputable professional evidential medium to begin to connect with your loved one in spirit.

- Consider learning evidential mediumship to connect directly for yourself.

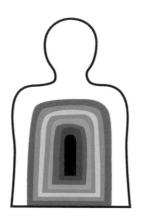

EIGHT

Building The Eighth Layer
Of RESILIENCE

Next level – greater understanding of personal development and experiences as a conscious being (mindset growth).

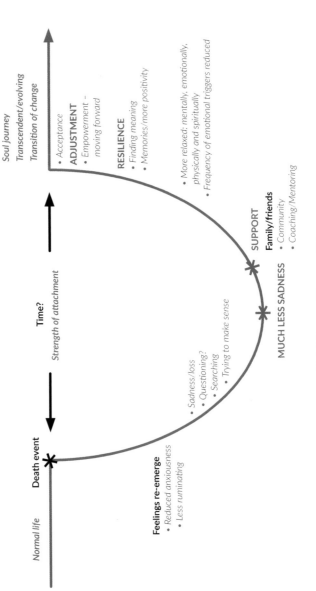

Grief Curve, Diagram 1D

By this stage in your self-help journey, you will hopefully be feeling better about yourself. Each layer of resilience you build is intended to fill the hole left by your loss more and more with good self-nourishment and personal development.

As you move through the Grief Curve, Diagram 1D, you may find yourself embracing the transition and perhaps even going beyond what you have previously known. That is not to say you won't swing back and forth in the Grief Curve at times when your loss is triggered, but as your resilience builds, memories of your loved one will become happier and fill your heart with fondness and warmth. You may have already experienced this, in which case you will be feeling the shift from pain and suffering to acceptance and ease.

In this chapter, I will be helping you to explore deep within yourself, consciously and energetically. I ask you to keep an open mind about the new learnings I am offering you, as this and the remaining chapters of the book take you and your higher consciousness and energy awareness to the next level, and onwards. I will offer you suggestions to help you achieve this, should you wish to do so.

What is consciousness?

Grief challenges you to think, feel and experience beyond your 'normal' understandings and awareness about yourself and life. It forces you out of your comfort zones to explore other dimensions, which may previously have been completely unknown to you. Without talking about it or studying it, you may never have made sense of the natural psychological development that comes from grief. You may not even have been conscious of it. It is interesting that academics and specialists in this area of work suggest less than 5% of the global population live consciously or are conscious beings.[22]

This is important. Because our world is changing so rapidly, we need more people living consciously for it and humanity to survive.

What is living consciously?

Richard Barrett speaks of seven levels of consciousness[23] which go beyond Maslow's hierarchy of needs, beyond self-actualisation. He substitutes 'hierarchy of needs' with 'states of consciousness', and each state of consciousness is defined by specific values and behaviours:

---

22 R Kegan, *In Over Our Heads: Mental demands of modern life* (Harvard University Press, 1995)
23 Barrett Values Centre,' The Barrett Model™', www.valuescentre.com/barrett-model

- Level 1 is survival – satisfying your psychological needs by learning how to stay alive, keep fit and healthy, and staying free from harm.

- Level 2 is relationships, conforming – keeping safe and nurtured by those around you via being loyal to your family, friends, colleagues and culture.

- Level 3 is self-esteem, differentiating – finding ways to be admired and recognised by your family and peers by excelling at what you do best.

- Level 4 is transformation, individuating – letting go of aspects of your parental and cultural conditioning that prevent you from becoming who you really are.

- Level 5 is internal cohesion, self-actualising – becoming fully who you are by finding your sense of purpose and leading a values-driven life.

- Level 6 is making a difference, integrating – aligning with others who share your values and purpose to make a difference in the world.

- Level 7 is service – fulfilling your destiny by leaving a legacy and using your gifts in service to the world.[24]

---

24 R Barrett, 'Levels of Consciousness', Barret Academy for the Advancement of Human Values, undated, www.barrettacademy. com/levels-of-consciousness

Perhaps you can identify where you are presently. I like to see myself at Level 6 as I am in service to others while transforming myself in grief. I'm consciously aware while continuing to evolve and change.

Living consciously is about becoming and remaining aware that all things are interconnected. All life, each and every being and the earth itself, is a living, breathing organism. Everything is dependent on everything else as a huge global ecosystem. Everything is energy which vibrates at its own specific frequency.

As we grow and develop psychologically, mentally and emotionally, we are vibrating at different frequencies at different stages in our lives. Consequently, we all have the potential to move from three-dimensional to five-dimensional beings. Living three dimensionally, we are not aware of the many different consciousness layers and energetic levels we are made up of as multi-dimensional beings. That is living five dimensionally, with all its benefits.

Looking at the seven levels of consciousness, we can see how each level is like a stage that correlates to our age development from younger years into older years, but mental, emotional and spiritual intelligence can be gained at any age through good education and personal development. This is exciting. Learning, growing and expanding our consciousness happens organically when we are experiencing the right conditions, such as being surrounded by a healthy environment, both at home and socially, and being with like-minded people who encourage and support each other to grow consciously.

The more developed we become, the more we recognise there are conscious people on this planet, and the more conscious our populations become.

How to develop consciousness

We are born with an innate ability to survive. It's all about 'me'. Being completely dependent, we have to find ways to get all our physical needs met from our primary care givers.

At level 2, we learn to become 'we'. We adapt to become social beings; to fit into family structures and social environments; to be accepted and loved.

At level 3, we learn that by being good at something, we can gain approval and admiration from our family and peers. From this, we get our self-esteem.

When we start to transform, we learn that all the things we have done until now have been attached to conditions that no longer serve us. These actions, behaviours and beliefs prevent us from being our authentic selves, who we are uniquely. This is when transformation takes place, so that the next levels move us beyond that to a higher consciousness.

At level 5, we learn that self-actualising is becoming all that we can be and living our life with purpose and meaning. In counselling, this is what clients achieve through personal therapy, making choices for change that promote their progress and advancement. This may involve changing a job, studying or training, a new career, starting a business or restructuring the one they have.

Integrating is when we decide to make changes in our lives that enable us to surround ourselves with like-minded people who share our values and beliefs. During this process of consciously taking life-fulfilling decisions to make a difference, we will be led to find out or confirm what our destiny is. We are all born to live out our purpose.

Finally, we learn that serving others is the continuation of integration as we live out our destinies. How will we know? We will feel it in our spirit and soul. When we feel aligned with our bodies and mind, we are at ease and contented throughout our whole being. As we live out our soul journey in whatever service we offer to others using our unique gifts, we are fulfilling our destiny, leaving our legacy, being fully aware, fully conscious that the meaning and purpose of this life is love and healing. We all have a place in that. I wonder, what is yours?

All learning is about raising consciousness. Education is empowering, and here you are working your way through the next level of consciousness with me.

Higher consciousness frequencies

People who have a higher consciousness operate at a higher frequency than others. David Hawkins, MD, PhD, scientist, experienced clinician, university lecturer and author of several books, is a widely known authority within the field of conscious research. In one of his insightful books *Power vs Force*,[25] which I referenced in Chapter Five, he talks about the energetic struggle between force and dominance as opposed to power and consciousness.

Hawkins devised a map of consciousness that determines the energetic vibrational level (measured in Hertz) at which you are living given each situation and emotion you are feeling. The map illustrates how grief vibrates at 75 while love vibrates at 500. Joy vibrates at 540 and peace vibrates at 600. The highest of all is enlightenment, vibrating at 700–1,000. This is known as pure consciousness. The kind of people who reach these heightened levels are the great spiritual leaders and teachers associated with the Divine such as Jesus, Krishna, Buddha and the saints who operate from unconditional love.[26]

Hawkins explains that the main element of this higher level of consciousness is love: a love that is unconditional and permanent; a love that doesn't change

25 D Hawkins, *Power vs. Force* (2014, Hay House)
26 https://veritaspub.com/map-of-consciousness/

because there are no longer any outside influences to change it. This love comes from the heart, not from or affected by the mind. It is pure love with the power to positively help and influence others.

The vibration of love, this heart-centred intuitive frequency, rises higher as unconditional love and compassion progresses through the levels of joy and peace.[27]

The impact of higher levels of personal consciousness on business

By loving unconditionally, we are in the business of doing sacred work while being in service to others. As we become more heart centred, this will inevitably change the way we conduct our business, which is explained in Ken Wilber's Summary of Spiral Dynamics model.[28] He says that as we become more heart-centred beings by the process of widening our conscious interconnectivity, we naturally ensure our business becomes more heart centred, too, making a paradigm shift from decades of competitive models to cooperation and collaboration.

---

27 D Hawkins, *Power vs. Force* (2014, Hay House)
28 K Wilber, 'Summary of Spiral Dynamics model', https://awaken. com/2014/04/ken-wilber-summary-of-spiral-dynamics-model/

Lifting your energetic vibrations

To help you along the journey of taking your consciousness to the next level, these suggestions will lift your energetic vibrations. They will enable you to learn to be fully self-reliant, self-sufficient and live by self-resilience. Make a choice to:

- Take action, be proactive

- Own raising your own frequencies

- Seek solutions, be inquisitive and curious

- Take responsibility, for yourself first and foremost

- Be accountable, have integrity, be honest

- See possibilities, be open minded

- Find better ways to live, be eclectic in your choices

- Be hopeful, optimistic

Energy-boosting methods to help you

Here are some energy-boosting methods you can use to assist you in this process:

- Crystals – learn about them and have them on you or around you every day in some way. They contain natural energies that raise your energy when you are connected to them. For crystals that can help with grief, download a free document from my website. www.joysackettwood.com

- Energy healing treatment methods, as explained in Layer Five – have regular sessions with a well-qualified practitioner or learn these methods for yourself. Use reiki, EFT/tapping and acupressure.

- Chakra and aura clearing and cleansing – learn to do this for yourself through meditation and visualisation techniques.

- Sound healing – sound baths using gongs, sound forks, shamanic drumming, either live or online. Use these on a regular basis. Sound baths are created by striking gongs, brass bowls, crystal bowls and tuning forks. The practitioner leads a sound meditation using these instruments to produce vibrational waves that wash over and through you to bring about a deep sense of inner peace and calm. Many people find it incredibly soothing and following the session will have a deep sense of having cleared, cleansed and balanced their energy fields, which is positively uplifting and refreshing.

- Chanting – voice sound vibrations from the heart with love intentions.

- Meditation – practise and experience various techniques for ten to twenty minutes daily.

- Tai chi, qigong, yoga – learn how energy flows within you and around you with gentle body movements, paying attention to promoting good health holistically.

Universal energy is a proven healing life force known as chi, ki or prana in Eastern traditions and as spirit energy in Western religious traditions. Also known as Orinda by the Iroquois people, this Divine Source is believed to be energetically present and accessible in every human being, no matter what cultural and religious community we live in.

You may be interested in listening to a TEDx Talk on Theory U which explains the various conscious levels and energetic vibrations of listening.[29] This encourages an open mind, open heart and open will to transform consciousness into emerging new futures for all. By affecting your future, it has an impact on the wider community's future, the nation's future and the global future, as well as positively influencing the natural environment and all other aspects of humanity, animals, plants and creatures.

Integrated beings

Our physical body is a vessel, a container, a conduit for our spiritual energy. It may help you to look at these diagrams:

---

29 O Scharmer, 'Theory U – Learning from the future as it emerges' (TEDx Talk, 2016), www.youtube.com/watch?v=GMJefS7s3lc

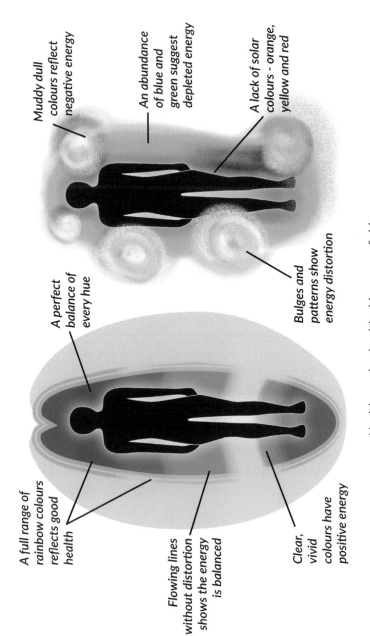

Muddy dull colours reflect negative energy

An abundance of blue and green suggest depleted energy

A lack of solar colours - orange, yellow and red

A perfect balance of every hue

Bulges and patterns show energy distortion

A full range of rainbow colours reflects good health

Flowing lines without distortion shows the energy is balanced

Clear, vivid colours have positive energy

Healthy and unhealthy bio-energy fields

Energy centre	What it controls	Element	Crystal/stone	Physical connections
Crown chakra I understand	Our ability to be fully connected spiritually	Divine consciousness	Clear quartz	Pineal gland, brain, nervous system, whole body
Third eye chakra I see	Our ability to focus on and see the bigger picture	Light	Amethyst	Pituitary gland, head, eyes and face
Throat chakra I talk	Our ability to communicate	Sound/music	Aquamarine	Thyroid, vocal chords, metabolism, ears, nose, mouth, teeth and neck
Heart chakra I love	Our ability to love	Air	Rose quartz	Thymus, heart, lungs, immune system, upper back, arms and hands
Solar plexus chakra I do	Our ability to be confident and in control of our lives	Fire	Amber	Spleen, gall bladder, liver, pancreas, middle back
Sacral chakra I feel	Our connection to and ability to accept others and new experiences	Water	Tiger's eye	Sexual organs, reproductive system, lower digestive organs, bladder, lower back
Root/base chakra I am	Represents our foundation and sense of being grounded	Earth	Hematite	Kidneys, adrenals, hips, legs, feet

Chart of the chakras and their connection to the physical body

When we become truly integrated beings, we are aware that our mind, body, emotions and spirit are all interconnected and in balance with each other. We also become more aware of others around us, how they affect us and how we affect them. In other words, we become consciously conscious. We have an inner knowing that we are connected to life in all its forms: all the creatures of earth, sky and ocean, trees and plants, even the earth itself and the greater universe beyond. It follows, then, that the more conscious we become, the more holistically we will think.

Thoughts as energy influencing our wellbeing

In his award-winning book *The Biology of Belief*,[30] Bruce H Lipton, PhD provides a fascinating scientific study with convincing evidence on how the biochemical effects of the brain's functioning show all the cells of our body are affected by our thoughts, and thoughts can actually change our DNA. Positive thinking creates healthy cells and negative thinking creates unhealthy ones.

This breakthrough evidence and knowledge will enable complementary healthcare businesses to flourish and establish more holistic practices, giving people more confidence to engage in alternative therapies. In my

---

30   BH Lipton, *The Biology of Belief: Unleashing the power of consciousness, matter and miracles* (Hay House, 2015)

experience, people have either become mistrusting of traditional medical care that leans far too heavily on the pharmaceutical industry, or become too reliant on it. Either way, now that you are more informed, you can make the choices you want for yourself, and with choice comes empowerment.

The COVID-19 pandemic revealed how important it is to raise our consciousness to the next level. Many people were forced into experiencing life differently throughout the lockdown, seeing it from a different perspective. Coping with the enforced situation impacted on them personally – physically, mentally, emotionally and spiritually – bringing about a shift in personal consciousness, the collective consciousness of wider communities, nations and the world, and inevitably the universal consciousness, too.

It was interesting to follow social media during lockdown. I observed how people were shaken out of their personal bubbles, woken up, reconnecting to other people around them. They faced up to the reality of what is important and what is not in the world, becoming more conscious of what has been happening to the environment. The positive consequence of less pollution and industry was so noticeable, and the impact of this awareness on environmental, global, sociological, economic and political issues couldn't be ignored, all working towards the greater consciousness of which you, I and the next generation are a part.

PERSONAL EXPERIENCE

Since the death of my son, Jack, my own conscious levels have been raised substantially. Not only have I become more aware of the impact of grief on a much deeper personal level, I have learnt a lot from the books I have read, the research for this book and the people I have spoken to for the case studies. This grief, unlike any other I have experienced, has been an education in itself, and this is the difference Jack's death has made to me.

As an educator/ teacher, I am aware that education is all about raising consciousness, and that knowledge and understanding bring power. This has helped me a lot. I think differently, I feel differently. Jack's death and the education I have gained as a result have changed me on every level. My consciousness has been enriched and strengthened. As a woman, I have become more reflective and insightful, having learnt much more about myself and my capabilities, as well as being more connected and empathic to others who have had a child die. I have become more conscious of love – the power of love, its purpose, and that love is actually what life is all about.

Suggestions to help you

- Learn what consciousness really is and how to live consciously.

- Become consciously aware of raising your consciousness.

- Make a copy of the list of 'choices' to lift your energetic vibrations and keep them near to you in your work or home space to focus on and practise.

- Engage in energy-boosting techniques.

- Engage in holistic therapies and treatments.

- Understand how your thoughts can influence your wellbeing.

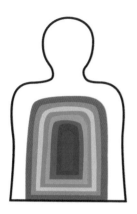

NINE

Building The Ninth Layer Of RESILIENCE

Change – this covers transition, spiritual interconnections, advancement, new paradigms, a different relationship with your loved one (spiritual growth).

It's probably quite clear to you by now that your grief and the death of your loved one has changed you and will continue to do so; that you and your life will never be the same again. I have written this book specifically to help you with managing the changes and adapting to a new life without your loved one being in it physically.

This chapter is about exploring these changes, helping you to understand the many different aspects and dynamics of change on the Grief Curve, Diagram 1D and how they relate to you personally. We will consider the various ideas and beliefs regarding the afterlife and the changes your loved one is experiencing. Then I will offer some suggestions to assist you in embracing the changes you choose to make to take you further along your personal soul journey, continuing through your transition following the physical death of your loved one from living a three-dimensional existence to a five-dimensional one.

Change is inevitable

The concept of impermanence forms the basis of the teachings of Buddhism. When we as individuals alter our conscious awareness, change will happen within our society and expand into the wider world and universal consciousness.

PERSONAL EXPERIENCE

I have been changed from feeling powerless over the situation of Jack dying to finding the power within it. I have the power of choice (as we all do) to allow this unwelcome intrusion into my life either to shrink me or to expand me as a human being. I have made the choice to embrace it and use it to the best of my ability, to experience and learn from it for the purpose of my own personal growth, focusing on my conscious expansion and the evolution of my soul for the benefit of others in my work and life in the hope and belief it will help me to be a better person. I have developed psychically/ spiritually from experiencing the transformational power of grief and loss.

I have shifted through the process of what happened 'to me' to what now happens 'through me'. This is in tune with my ultimate life's purpose: being in the service of others and living a heart-centred energetically aligned life that's uplifting and fulfilling with meaning and purpose. And, of course, my exciting new relationship with Jack has truly changed me.

Other influences of change

Aside from personal grief at the loss of a loved one, we see changes happening in our lives at a rapid rate due to the technological age we live in. Never before in the history of the world have things moved at such a high pace. What was new yesterday will have been upgraded or become obsolete by tomorrow.

We all feel the stress of this change in our lives, yet most of us cannot live without it. Our online presence is imperative. It supports the financial survival of all businesses and keeps us up to date with what owners, leaders and employees are doing in our industry. It's how we reach out for services and products in an instant on our phones.

Adapting to and learning a constant stream of new information has never been so demanding. It is children and young people who are the 'experts' of change as their brains are wired for absorbing knowledge like a sponge. As the generation of change, they will be the future leaders. Education has a massive responsibility to uphold for our children, and the survival of the planet. Therefore, we must all be conscious of our own and human evolution. This inevitably brings change.

Therapeutic change

When clients first come to me, some have said, 'Can I really change? After all, a leopard cannot change its spots, can it?' Of course we can change – the business I have is all about personal development and therapeutic change. We *do* have the power to change.

CASE STUDY: ANXIETY AND POOR CONFIDENCE

One client suffered from anxiety and low self-esteem since childhood. She had tried many 'remedies' in an attempt to balance the never-ending uncertainties in her life.

Through therapy, she gained an understanding of
the yin and yang in life; the dark and the bright
complimenting each other during life's challenges.

Her newfound confidence and the use of learned
techniques allow her to achieve her goals and speak up
when needed, all contributing to a profound lifelong
effect on her emotional wellbeing.

Therapeutically, we change when the pain of not
doing so becomes greater than the pain of doing so.
Symbolically, we are like an acorn. All the potential of
an oak tree exists within; the acorn just needs the right
conditions to achieve this potential. I wonder, does a
caterpillar actually know it will eventually become a
butterfly? These changes in nature require shifts in
conscious existence, as change does within you and me.
Your potential to be all that you can be is truly magical,
just like the two examples from nature. After all, we
humans are part of nature.

Courage to change

As human beings, we need change. We need to transform ourselves, otherwise life becomes too rigid,
restricted, resistance based and boring. Of course, at
times embracing change means we have to be brave
and open to new ideas, new ways of doing things, a
new way of life. Sometimes it can feel a bit scary, but
with fear comes excitement. Accepting and embracing

change is exciting, and with this excitement we can feel energised and strong.

A courageous person enters into a challenging situation without knowing what the outcome will be. Taking small steps to expand your comfort zone, even if you initially feel uncomfortable, will be a massive confidence boost and feel incredibly empowering. A book I have recommended to many clients over the years is *Feel the Fear and Do it Anyway* by Susan Jeffers.[31] She writes so well about how she overcame her own fears and anxieties by being brave and coming out of her comfort zone to recreate herself and enhance her life. This self-help book is loaded with valuable help and support, exercises and suggestions.

The commitment to change requires courage, but the rewards are beneficial and powerful. Fear carries a low vibration, while courage carries a high vibration. By embracing and accepting change with all its many layers of growth, you are raising your energetic vibrations and living a healthier life, naturally boosting your immune system with the surge of endorphins and serotonins that accompany the feeling of accomplishing personal success.

Being courageous means knowing yourself, letting go, making decisions to make changes. It requires

---

31 S Jeffers, *Feel the Fear and Do it Anyway: How to turn your fear and indecision into confidence and action* (Vermillion, 2007)

your attention and awareness, focusing your conscious intention to follow through with the change.

According to my friend Grace Chatting of WWMB, everyday courage can be divided into four groups:

- Moral courage – doing what we believe to be right.

- Disciplined courage – steadfast believing for the greater good.

- Intellectual courage – maturity of new learnings, understandings and insights.

- Empathic courage – a knowledge of personal bias. Being able to enjoy other people's successes and engage in their situations from their point of view.

Becoming our true selves and all that we can be is courageous. Learning to live without fear of judgement or criticism from others and accepting ourselves as we are is truly living in a place of peace and contentment from within. When we push our own boundaries with an open mind, we open up limitless possibilities for ourselves.

Just think of the amazing true stories you may have read or heard about people overcoming extreme adversity, physical injuries and illnesses, defeating all the odds. The tremendous inner strength and determination of these remarkable people, such as motivational speakers

Helen Keller and Nick Vujicic, inspire the belief that anything is possible. I suggest you watch any of their YouTube videos and Podcasts to be inspired.

And so it is. The power is within you. How remarkable it is to discover you are far more than meets the eye, a truly multi-dimensional being.

Historical change

People once believed the world is flat because that was what they were told. Even when it was proven scientifically that the world is round, some people didn't want to change their views and hung on to the old belief because they feared change, didn't want to be in the minority and risk being unaccepted by the majority. History is rife with people being persecuted and even executed for having supported enlightened beliefs.

It is helpful to note that all the major religions were founded by great teachers who ushered in new spiritual and philosophical reforms in the context of the historical times they lived in. And today, there are still great spiritual teachers and reformers within all the world's religions. In essence, all religions express the love and life force of a god in this particular existence on earth. The metaphors and symbolism within religious traditions are hugely empowering, each playing a part in our understanding of the universal consciousness.

New ideas and changes from inventions, philosophies, religions and society challenged the established order of the times. Inevitably, what people knew and believed in the Middle Ages was different to what people knew and believed in Elizabethan times, which in turn was different to what people knew and believed in Victorian times, and so on into the twenty-first century. Each age and historical stage can be distinguished by its changes in travel, industry and political conflict. It stands to reason the old belief system would eventually be taken over by the new belief system of evolved conscious thinkers, until that in turn is replaced by another wave of new ideas and beliefs.

The unhealthy effect of change

Our present technological age has taken over from the industrial age. How different your life is from your parents' and grandparents' thanks to labour-saving devices providing opportunities and positive changes in education, work and social fluidity. The invention of computers and the World Wide Web has enabled us to become a global community. We can get information about anything at a touch of a button. We get instant news and can voice opinions on social media. We have the availability of information overload, so much so that we are bombarded with stimuli and are at risk of being over stimulated, which isn't healthy.

Add to this the fast pace and demands of the modern world, creating much stress and anxiety. It is no wonder there is so much concern about the number of mental-health problems people are experiencing, which are growing globally at an alarming rate.

Changing attitudes to redress this overwhelm come from the holistic health sector. This sees and advocates the need for people to slow down in general and take the time they require for silence and contemplation.

Change as peace in life

Silence and contemplation are key in promoting peace. It is in the meditative peace of our lives that we give our thinking mind a rest, recharge our energies, relax and calm our nervous system. It enhances reflective thinking, changing our brainwaves from beta to alpha, which means we become more receptive to inspired thoughts. Changing our conscious states of mind also enables us to experience expanded perspectives of knowingness.

This state of deeper/ higher consciousness, which many call the spiritual, intuitive, transcendental, mindfulness, etc, is a great practice to engage in as it will enable you to focus on aspects of yourself and life in a gentle and compassionate way. People who are disciplined in this practice are able to go quickly into a meditative state, seeking and receiving answers and solutions to challenges they are experiencing.

Changing your beliefs about the afterlife

Scientific studies can help us to make sense of things regarding the possibility of an afterlife. Evidence changes thoughts and beliefs.

You may have wondered about and questioned:

- Near death experiences (NDEs)
- Reincarnation
- Heaven or Hell

NDEs

Many people believe they have had an NDE in that they have clinically died and have had an experience that took them out of their physical bodies and into a different place of consciousness, existence or reality. Common characteristics are:

- Seeing their own body at the point of death
- Observing the behaviours of others around them
- Being aware of consequential events happening

- Hearing conversations that they shouldn't have been able to hear in rational terms

- Being drawn down a tunnel to a bright light

- Being met by deceased family members

- A sense of happiness and joy, peace

- Feeling no pain; all physical suffering ceasing

- Hearing beautiful music or singing

- Having meaningful conversations with and gaining insights from relatives who have 'passed over'

- Seeing their lives flashing before their eyes like a video in which they review their soul's journey without judgement as an experience of learning in the presence of pure love

- Feeling they are pulled back into their bodies with a jerk when they return to this existence

NDEs are characteristically life-changing experiences. Afterwards, many people report a new or renewed interest in spirituality and humanity. Interestingly, these experiences are similar across all cultures, religious beliefs and societies throughout the world.

Evidence for NDEs

I understand that in hospitals and care homes, doctors, nurses and staff are familiar with NDEs as common occurrences. According to researcher Dr Ken Ring, PhD, there have been tens of thousands of evidentiary cases recorded by doctors and university professors.[32] This data is strong evidence that there is a continuation of consciousness after the death of the physical body.

Many individuals have written accounts of their NDEs as they were so profoundly powerful. When I was a secondary school teacher of religious education, my students absolutely loved hearing such stories. They helped to open up conversations on the metaphysical aspects of life and death, which fascinated us all.

One powerful story was by Lesley Joan Lupo, in which she told how she'd died for fourteen minutes having been stampeded by horses. As the title of her book *Remember, Every Breath is Precious: Dying taught me how to live*[33] indicates, this was certainly a life-changing experience for her.

Give consideration to stories and first-hand accounts of NDEs. They can bring you comfort and reassurance

---

32   K Ring, *Lessons from the Light* (Insight Books, 1998)
33   LJ Lupo, *Remember, Every Breath is Precious: Dying taught me how to live* (White Crow Books, 2018)

regarding where your loved one is and what has happened to them.

Reincarnation

Another traditional concept is the belief in reincarnation. This belief is mostly held by Eastern religious traditions such as Hinduism, Buddhism and Sikhism, but many people, across all faiths or none, believe that when we die, after a period of time, we are reborn again into this world.

The purpose of reincarnation varies across beliefs and cultures. In Hinduism, it is associated with the law of Karma and the caste system by way of reward or punishment according to your behaviour in this life. In Buddhism, it is the continuation of the development of your consciousness to finally become enlightened like the Buddha. It is similar in Sikhism.

In other spiritual learnings, reincarnation is connected to fulfilling your soul journey. Each life is agreed upon between you and your higher spiritual guides and masters in association with the Divine Source.

Evidence for reincarnation

This is another area of discussion my religious education students found fascinating, again creating much interesting debate. The convincing factors are when people are able to recall in detail past-life experiences of living with other families, being known by different names, living in countries they've never visited in this lifetime, speaking languages they've never learnt, knowing information that can only be backed up by archives and museums. This recall is predominantly done under hypnosis with experienced practitioners.

One documented source of this kind of information comes from Dr Brian Weiss. He details his research with his clients in his books *Same Soul, Many Bodies*[34] and *Many Lives, Many Masters*.[35]

Some people have argued that hypnosis may not be the best evidence for reincarnation and past-life memories as people could make them up, but many hypnotherapists say that the evidence that comes directly from the person under hypnosis includes their emotional and bodily responses that accompany their recollections. These are hard to deny rationally. Scientist Dr Helen Wambach, PhD conducted research on data collected from 1,088 case studies of people recalling past lives under hypnosis and found that only eleven of the total contained discrepancies. She concluded that the data supported actual past-life recall, accurately reflecting the real past rather than representing fantasies.[36]

---

34   B Weiss, *Same Soul, Many Bodies* (Piatkus, 2004)
35   B Weiss, *Many Lives, Many Masters: The true story of a prominent psychiatrist, his young patient and the past-life therapy that changed both their lives* (Piatkus, 1994)
36   H Wambach, *Reliving Past Lives* (Bantam Books 1979) p28

Over the years, I have borne witness to past-life stories that were not recalled through hypnosis, which tells me that some people have vivid recollections of past lives that they don't often get the opportunity to talk about.

CASE STUDY: RICHARD

When Jack was ten years old, he had a good friend, Richard, who lived a few doors down from us. Richard's parents took him to Germany to visit the Army camp his dad had been stationed in at one time. On arrival in Germany, they hired a car to tour the area.

Richard had been looking out the car window for a while when he asked his mum and dad if they were going to visit his 'other mum and dad who live here'. When they questioned him, he directed them to an area his dad had never heard of before and pointed to a house.

'There, that's where I used to live,' he said. They became convinced Richard was recalling a previous life as they had no other explanation for what he was talking about so sincerely.

PERSONAL EXPERIENCE

As a child aged about six, I remember having a lucid experience, perhaps a dream, in which I found myself in a beautiful garden. This was a most unusual experience for me, yet the place seemed familiar. Arches were covered in pink roses and everything looked like it was from olden times. I saw people sitting around dressed in old-fashioned clothes, talking, sipping drinks. It was a warm, sunny day.

As I wandered around, I overheard someone say, 'She was a good woman' or something like that, and I suddenly realised he was talking about me. The people were gathered together for a reason connected to me. It seemed odd.

'I am here,' I said, but nobody seemed to hear me. I then realised they couldn't see me, either, and wondered why. They seemed to like me, though, and spoke of me kindly.

This 'dream' has stayed with me and remains vivid today. As I've got older, I've realised the clothes the people wore were in the style of the eighteenth century, as was the layout of the beautiful garden. Over time, I've got the sense I was attending my own funeral gathering.

Déjà vu is another way of understanding time in a different reality.

PERSONAL EXPERIENCE

I remember an incident when I took my younger brother to the post office to open up his first savings account. Mark was aged about six at the time, but I remember the conversation so clearly. He asked me how much the savings account would cost him. Being only twelve years old myself, I remember laughing and telling him it didn't cost him anything. For some reason, I knew how the conversation would start and end, even as I was engaging in it.

Some people say déjà vu is evidence of reincarnation and we have lived the experience before. Others say it is evidence of time slips, as in quantum physics, or a parallel reality in that we live several lives all at the same time.

Hell, the evidence

In my studies and work, I have heard of several people having had a past life or NDE, but few have referred to experiencing an actual place called 'Hell' as taught in the Western religions such as Christianity. Critics and cynics say the fear of Hell ensures social control and religious conformity. The Catholic tradition often comes under the same kind of bad press as any religious fundamentalism and judgementalism for overemphasising Hell.

I learnt a lot about Hell when I belonged to a Pentecostal Evangelical church and a Charismatic Free church, as Hell is an integral part of the faith, doctrines and beliefs of these churches. From my theological studies and personal explorations, I understand Hell to be a state of mind, and that it can be experienced in the here and now. We can create our own Hell by the choices we make and the lives we lead. After all, why would an all-loving, compassionate, nurturing God send you to Hell?

Heaven, the evidence

Heaven is traditionally the opposite to Hell. There are many referrals to Heaven as a place of bliss reported in accounts of NDEs, and evidential mediumship shows it as a place of pure love, joy and peace. Mediums have the ability to speak on behalf of people who have died and no longer exist in their physical forms. Countless stories from spirit people refer to their new existence as being in a place of unconditional love, acceptance and understanding, which is a 'state of Heaven' where there is no judgement.

Personal experience as evidence

In this section, I have summarised what the people I interviewed for this book told me they have experienced since the death of their loved one. It is interesting that they've all had a spiritual experience in some way or another. These are just some examples of ways your loved ones in spirit may find to communicate to you.

They felt/feel their loved one's spirit presence around them:

- 'I know they are still with me as I can feel them near me.'

- 'I often feel my hand being touched; I know it is my mum.'

Particular smells:

- 'I can smell their perfume/ cigarette smoke (if they were a smoker), etc.'

- 'I frequently smell her favourite flowers.'

Objects moving:

- 'My keys were in a strange place, not where I left them.'

- 'His photo on the wall often tilts.'

Signs:

- 'Whenever I see a robin, I think it is my mum coming to visit.'

- 'When a heart appears, I know it is my son letting me know he is near.'

- 'White feathers turn up in random places. I know she has sent them.'

Music:

- 'I switch on the radio and hear a song that has a strong connection to Dad.'

- I keep hearing her favourite song in my mind, over and over again.'

Electronics:

- 'My kettle keeps switching on and off.'

- 'My computer does random things at times; I just know it's my husband.'

- 'The frequency of the station on my radio gets tuned out at times.'

- 'The TV came on by itself.'

- 'The front doorbell keeps ringing and no one is there.'

CASE STUDY: VICKI

Vicki told me she had been driving in her car on Father's Day thinking about her husband who had died eighteen months previously. She had a memory of an occasion when they were out socially and he sang a particular karaoke song. She said it was so awful and embarrassing but the memory made her smile. At that moment the very song came on the radio. She looked up into her car mirror and behind her saw her husband's old car that had been sold.

Vicki was amazed by these 'weird' experiences, yet told me she felt calm and comforted by them too. She just knew it was her husband in spirit with her.

These signs are usually received well by the recipients, who say they feel a strong sense of peace and love that brings them comfort. Spiritual signs are experienced by people of all ages, although children are particularly receptive, from all walks of life, social statuses, cultures and races. Even the most logical of people can have unexplainable experiences.

I have experienced all of these signs and more from my son Jack. In truth, I am still adapting to the change in our relationship, which continually fascinates, delights and amazes me. Jack, too, has changed so much since becoming a spirit person.

Another direct method of communication seems to be by way of dreaming.

Dreams as evidence

People tell me they have had significant dreams following the death of their loved one. These are usually vivid dreams in which their loved one brings them a message of comfort and reassurance. Often, they say that they are OK and happy where they are, out of all pain and suffering. The people experiencing the dream tend to say their loved one looks younger, physically well and healthy, no matter what caused their death. This generally brings a great sense of peace and comfort, both during the dream and on awakening. I have written a short blog on the therapeutic value of dreams and hypnotherapy which you can find on my website. www.swanstherapy.co.uk

It is great to know that changes in science and technology are playing a vital prominent role in ushering in the new paradigm of understanding our evolving consciousness, spirituality and life in the hereafter. This evolution – which we will cover in the final chapter – is going to alter the way we think about life and death forever.

Suggestions to help you

- Understand that change is inevitable and can be therapeutic.

- Consider what you are prepared to change in yourself and for your life. Make a list of how you may be able to make those changes. What will the outcome be for you in making those changes?

- Change takes courage, but it is through being brave that we grow mentally, emotionally and spiritually.

- Make sure you avoid the negative effects of the fast rate of change in the modern world by taking the time to slow down and reflect in peace and silence.

- Examine the evidence in favour of an afterlife. What is your experience of phenomena such as inexplicable signs and déjà vu?

TEN

Building The Tenth Layer
Of RESILIENCE

Evolution – evidence of the continuing soul journey and a release from **hole** (feeling hollow) to feeling **whole** on each level. Conscious awareness of being a multi-dimensional vibrational-energy being (energy growth).

This is the truly transformative layer of RESILIENCE.

As you are probably aware by now, personal development and soul evolution are an experience of constantly growing and changing (see Grief Curve,

Diagram 1D). As we continue to learn, we realise there is so much more to know and life gives us even more challenges to master. You may like to take a moment to reflect on how your new awareness has already grown, developed and evolved through your personal grief journey.

To complete our journey together, I will present the exciting scientific evidence for continued consciousness I learnt while researching for this book. This was pure nourishment for my soul: proof there really is no such thing as death. How this may influence your grief, your view on life after death and your relationship with your loved one in spirit is, of course, for you to decide, but I truly hope what I am passing on to you will be worthy of serious consideration, bringing nourishment for your soul, too.

Technology and science as evidence

As part of the research I did for this book, I found some fascinating information regarding science and spirituality. Of particular interest was a YouTube video called 'The Dalai Lama and Quantum Physics'[37] in which the Dalai Lama listens to Anton Zeilinger discussing new ideas being developed and how knowledge is more fundamental than reality, reality being the material

---

37 A Zeilinger, 'The Dalai Lama and Quantum Physics' (2007), www. youtube.com/watch?v=U43pXuGhEg8

aspects of life. During the discussion, scientists conduct an experiment to show that since the 1920s, there has been an order in quantum physics due to the progress in technology that can prove a new picture of reality. They explain how quantum computers can provide more information than classic computers, and this information has thrown new light on understanding reality, the past and future, and the interconnectedness of our lives.

It was interesting to fast forward nine years to 2016, when the Dalai Lama held a series of discussions with neuroscientists at Mind & Life conference recorded on YouTube.[38] I was particularly fascinated by the exploration of reincarnates.

The discussion focused on consciousness surviving physical death, and concluded that the mind is separate from the brain, explaining that the brain is a material organ while the mind is a stream of consciousness which remains in a 'light body' after the physical body has ceased to function. In addition to this, energy is pure consciousness, and it is energy that enables our transition.

---

38 'What Is It That Reincarnates?' (September 2016), www.youtube.com/watch?v=vQ0CoQyIe7Y

Science and energy healing

Energy healing and energy treatments, which include acupuncture, acupressure, reiki, EFT, etc, influence our energy body, and science is now investigating these phenomena. These YouTube discussions confirmed for me that spirit – consciousness or mind – is the energy that promotes movement through the various levels of consciousness, while the soul is the essence of who we are.

Science and meditation

The study also backed up that we can train our conscious awareness through meditation. Because we empty our busy thinking mind of everyday thoughts, the energy of the subtle mind becomes more evident. This is well practised by Buddhist monks and others who have mastered the skill of meditation.

Science and reincarnation

In respect to reincarnation, I learnt that memories of past lives are 'imprints' left in the stream of consciousness, so when somebody recalls a past life, either in its entirety or fragments, they are indeed recalling information in their conscious mind experiences. Quantum physics claims that when all the conditions are right, then a new material existence comes into being and we are reborn.

The Dalai Lama is convinced by the stories of young children who can recall past lives in remarkable detail for their present age, circumstances and experiences. Their memories are clear and personal, precise and convincing, and the information they share can often be validated through family members and research. Those who develop subtle minds, such as clairvoyants, psychics and mediums, are tuning in to true memories, according to this evidence-based debate.

Consciousness is everywhere in every living organism. Simple systems like plants have little consciousness, but complex systems like human beings have much more. One of the interesting questions raised by this knowledge is what happens to the consciousness, spirit, mind and soul of our loved one in between lives.

Life between lives

One of the most influential and respected research works done in this area was conducted by Michael Newton, PhD over several years of his lifetime. He documented many case studies in his book *Journey of Souls*,[39] and went on to detail even more case studies

---

39 M Newton, *Journey of Souls: Case studies of life between lives* (Llewellyn, 2004)

in his books *Destiny of Souls*,[40] *Life Between Lives*[41] and *Memories of the Afterlife*.[42] His recorded data shows remarkable similarities between the information people were able to give him about their soul experiences before being reborn again. The sheer mass of similar data from people across all cultures, faiths and beliefs validates evidence that consciousness, spirit and energy do continue after this particular physical material existence ceases, and confirms the rebirth into another physical material existence when the conditions are right.

His case studies reveal:

- What the death experience feels like

- What happens right after the death experience

- The learning that continues on the soul level

- Different levels of soul: new, intermediate and advanced

- The healing of the soul is the priority

- What happens to 'disturbed' souls in their healing

- There is no Hell

40   M Newton, *Destiny of Souls: New case studies of life between lives* (Llewellyn, 2001)
41   M Newton, *Life Between Lives: Hypnotherapy for spiritual regression* (Llewellyn, 2004)
42   M Newton, *Memories of the Afterlife: Life between lives stories of personal transformation* (Llewellyn, 2009)

- A feeling of complete acceptance

- Oneness with the ultimate Divine Source of all knowingness and absolute love

Divine Love, God, Source, Universal Consciousness, the Great Spirit, Higher Power, All Powerful One – whatever name you have attributed to the highest power of all, it is now referred to as the Field of Greatest Consciousness. For me, this is utterly fascinating and exciting, as it points definitively to the fact that this life is not the only reality that exists.

PERSONAL EXPERIENCE

When Jack died, I was able to ask him several questions about his death, his transition and what it was like for him. He communicated to me what he experienced and how loved ones in spirit came to meet him, and he was able to tell me some of the details I needed to know about the time leading up to his death, which brought me much comfort and relief.

About a month later, I decided to have a spiritual reading with Jennie McDowell, a good evidential medium, who told me Jack is happy and had been in training in the spirit world, and he is now busy working in a clinic – a rehab centre helping people with drug and alcohol addictions. He is also helping and supporting me with my healing and counselling work. She said he had been learning so fast in the spirit world, she was surprised at how strongly he was able to come through at this stage, communicating so well. Jack told her he was at peace and pointed at the coffin lid I had painted, and then laughed as he pointed to a halo above his head that went 'ping'.

'I am an angel now, Mum,' he said.

This was particularly poignant as he'd often said to me in life, 'I will never be an angel, Mum.' Jack had been quite a naughty person and we'd had a difficult relationship much of the time. This makes the way he has attained such an understanding about himself in the afterlife so amazing.

My relationship with Jack before he died

PERSONAL EXPERIENCE

Jack was a handsome, sensitive little boy, full of fun and laughter. He enjoyed playing with his friends and being active. I had been married to the father of Jack and his sister Jeneen for ten years. When this marriage didn't work out, Jeneen coped with the divorce much better than Jack. At the time, he was nine and Jeneen was seven.

As Jack grew older and became more and more troubled, our relationship became more challenging, which caused a lot of tension and strain. Jack and I clashed as much as we laughed. As mother and son, we had a relationship history that often felt to me like a battle of wills due to the different values we lived by, but over the years, no matter how angry we got with each other, we were always able to be forgiving. There was so much love between us. The physical distance didn't help as Jack had settled with his father in Devon and I lived in Dorset, but whenever we did get to see each other, it made us both really happy.

The information the evidential medium gave me was so clear and specific, I was left in no doubt it was my son speaking through her. In addition to this, I could really feel his presence, like a pleasant tingly pressure change in the air surrounding me. The blending of this with my own energy helped the communication to be strong and clear. This brought me great comfort, as well as intrigue, which set me on an investigation into what Jack is experiencing now in spirit, how he is doing between lives and how different he is.

Now I have developed my own spiritual/ psychic abilities during the times Jack and I have communicated, I hear great clarity and wisdom in his responses. In fact, he once told me, 'Ask me, Mum. Ask me anything – I am wise now'. When I asked him how he came be so wise, this was his reply that I found so deeply profound.

'There are no filters in the spirit realm. We will find, as time flows by, new ways of doing things. We communicate with our hearts, not with our minds. The heart is pure, the mind gets contaminated. The heart is "soul" – we are in soul talk now. Letting us know truths, being wise, being true, no need to sift out shit. It is all and real. It is what it is, no messing. All is good – love is what it is. Be kind – that is how it works here. We are talking through love, no mistakes, nothing to erase. Every word matters.'

Spiritual evidence

Confirmation of the presence of your loved one is reassuring, but some of you may doubt your experiences and dismiss them as 'hallucinations', the grief of bereavement playing tricks on your mind and emotions. Validation is important in our Western world of rational thinking and understanding, and I couldn't agree more, but as evolving individuals, we must be open to change of perspectives on all levels of consciousness and spirituality. Some people call this becoming 'awake'; an 'awakening experience'.

Power

We all have personal power to use for good, or not. A good definition of evil is the misuse of personal power.

As a multi-dimensional transformational human being myself, I have learnt we are forever expanding our awareness and energy. We have the individual power for good and, with the right intentions and attentions, to strengthen our personal power for service to others.

My personal spiritual evolution

One great source of positive influence for me in my new learnings through my grief journey came from a retired naval commander who's now an excellent evidential medium and teacher, Suzanne Giesemann.[43] I would recommend watching her YouTube videos, especially 'What our Loved Ones are Doing in the Afterlife'[44] and 'Your Place in The Cosmos Explained'.[45] I have attended two of her online courses, including an advanced one on evidential mediumship, which have taught and helped me so much. Through her reassurance and support, Suzanne has enabled me to develop my own mediumship skills and hone stronger communications with my son.

When my son died, it soon became clear to me that my relationship with him had not ended, merely changed. I remember someone saying to me at the time that I was just in denial about his death. For a while, I did wonder and question myself, but the evidence of my personal experiences unquestionably overrode this suggestion.

Scientific evidence for soul evolution

To satisfy my rational left brain, I decided to continue to seek scientific evidence. And in the same way as I was 'led to' Suzanne when I asked my son and team of

---

43 www.suzannegiesemann.com
44 S Giesemann, 'What our Loved Ones are Doing in the Afterlife' (2019), www.youtube.com/watch?v=J6fC1Z6kUZQ
45 S Giesemann, 'Your Place in The Cosmos Explained' (2020), www. youtube.com/watch?v=b9AURvWddA8

guides for the best teacher of mediumship to learn from, when I asked for the best scientific proof/ evidence available today to back up my confirmed belief that there is no such thing as death, Dr Gary E Schwartz, PhD, and Dr Mark Pitstick, MA, DC, came to my conscious attention.

Advanced research being undertaken by Dr Schwartz, a senior professor at the University of Arizona, where he is described as a clinically and spiritually minded scientist, and Dr Pitstick, a scientifically and spiritually minded clinician,[46] brought much strength to my convictions, and is the most exciting scientific evidence I have come across. They are creating an unprecedented paradigm shift in how we understand death with their amazing studies and evidence regarding spirituality, consciousness, existences beyond what we perceive this one to be and how life continues for people without material bodies, expanding communication with them.

Dr Schwartz and Dr Pitstick call people who have left this life post-material persons (PMPs) as they are still people, just without a 'suit of flesh'. The reality of this is clearly explained and documented with a vast amount of evidence in their book *Greater Reality Living*.[47] They make scientific concepts and the new 'language' used by living in a greater reality accessible to the

---

46 www.soulproof.com
47 MR Pitstick, GE Schwartz *Greater Reality Living: Integrating the evidence for eternal consciousness into your daily life* (CreateSpace, 2018)

layperson to help us make better sense of changes in our consciousness, while giving respectful credence to traditional religious teachings and cultures.

According to an article by Mark Pitstick, he identified that of the five senses we use (sight, sound, smell, taste and touch), presently we detect less than 1% of all that exists.[48] For example, what is visible to the eye is just a small fraction of the electromagnetic spectrum. They go on to say that the majority of life cannot be detected by our senses.

Reality is defined as the state of things that actually exist, and because so much escapes the senses, you and I have likely viewed life through a tiny pinhole – then questioned why things don't seem to make sense. 'Greater reality living' is a phrase coined by Dr Schwartz and Dr Pitstick to advocate that we can enjoy the existence of enhanced life by accepting and embracing the Field of Greater Consciousness in the here and now.

The benefits are:

- We eliminate the fear of death

- We enjoy a continued relationship with loved ones and pets

---

48 Mark Pitstick, 'How To See More of "The Big Picture of Life"', www. soulproof.com/see-big-picture-of-life/

- We become at one with the One and an integral part of the 'Greater Reality' perspective

- We receive assistance from guides, master teachers and higher energies

- We become interconnected with other people, animals, nature and all of life

- We have special purposes for experiencing being on this planet now

- We fulfil our destiny, our soul's purpose

- We are in service to others

Dr Schwartz and Dr Pitstick say that none of these benefits, which assist us to have a more joyful, peaceful and meaningful human experience, is apparent when we only rely on our five senses.

I too believe the benefits of lifting the veil could transform our lives wonderfully for the better. I would add these three attributes to Dr Schwartz and Dr Pitstick's list:

1. We grow in wisdom

2. We make an impact on the world, both in the here and now and in the next phase of life/lives

3. We become **whole**

Communicating, thriving and evolving

PERSONAL EXPERIENCE

Although I still miss my son in the physical at times, I feel my life has become so enriched by the journey his leaving has taken me on. I am grateful and happy to be able to communicate with him on a daily basis, to continue our relationship, which has deepened and improved radically. He is teaching me so much.

I have been told by other evidential mediums that Jack is a clever communicator and I am incredibly proud of him and the ways he is able to now offer me support and guidance. In addition, he has become my mediumship guide. I have been absolutely astonished at this phenomenon, which is beyond anything I could have ever imagined. My heart is filled to bursting as I write. I have become a Shining-Light parent, which means I have become the parent of a child that has transited to the greater reality. Through the experience of our new relationship I am transformed by the light of pure love and I am now supporting others to achieve this as a Shining-Light coach, which I love.

Apart from talking to Jack, I have learnt to talk on behalf of other people in spirit when they wish to send a loving message to somebody. Known as readings, these are intended to bring comfort and healing. Mediums who talk on behalf of your loved one have become super sensitive to higher energy vibrations. They are using more than just their five senses. Mediumship is like being a mediator or an interface for the communication, and exciting advancements mean technology may soon be able to do this, too.

The SoulPhone project

Dr Schwartz directs the SoulPhone project at the Laboratory for Advancements, University of Arizona.[49] There is excitement around the project, which will enable everyone and anyone to communicate with their loved PMPs in the greater reality, which Dr Schwartz and Dr Pitstick call the Field of all Possibilities. Together, they established The SoulPhone Foundation.

I find it so very exciting that this is happening in our lifetime!

Communicating with our loved one in spirit

If we wish to talk directly to our loved PMPs in the realm of greater reality/ consciousness, we must do so by increasing our energies. To meet up and achieve clearer conversations and images, we must raise our frequencies. Our material bodies are dense and naturally vibrate at a lower rate than those in spirit, who operate at a high frequency. To meet up and achieve

---

49   www.thesoulphonefoundation.org

clearer conversations and images, we need to balance those frequencies.

As multi-dimensional beings, we can decide *now* to live a five-dimensional life as opposed to a three-dimensional one – I have already offered suggestions on how to do this. Living in a higher frequency is healthy, positive and attracts fulfilment in the richness and diversities of life. Higher frequency feelings are emotions, and bring light, love and happiness. Remember, bodily sensations are your energy body, your aura/ bio-energy field, which expands with feelings related to the highest frequencies of love, peace and joy.

One of the main barriers to raising our energy is our own ego, so we must be mindful of this. Ego operates at a low vibration and gets in the way of high-energy living and our soul's progress.

Signs of the ego at work are:

- Living in three dimensions

- Pride/shame

- Anger

- Focus on self

- Un-forgiveness/bitterness

- Fear/doubt

- Worry

- Judgement

- Separation

Attributes of the soul are:

- Living in five dimensions

- Joy

- Peace

- Strength

- Courage

- Gratitude

- Humility

- Divine love

- Compassion

- A focus on service to others

You can learn to free yourself from allowing your ego to reduce your energy frequencies by becoming more self-reflective and aware. Matt Kahn's book, *Everything is Here to Help You*, referenced in Chapter Four, is a good place to start. Also, Barbara Marx

Hubbard's book *52 Codes for Conscious Self Evolution*,[50] co-created and edited by Carolyn Anderson, will be most helpful.

As you evolve personally, it is inevitable your views and approach to work and business will evolve, too. You'll experience a paradigm shift. Your integrity towards yourself and others – leaders, managers, employees, staff and colleagues – will increase massively. Your business plans and challenges will embrace a new holistic world view.

Relevant to this subject, I would recommend you watch a YouTube video by WWMB leader Grace Chatting, 'Why *Not* to Return to Business as Usual after the Coronavirus'.[51] In economics, it would make sense to be wise and follow the example of people leading the way in alternative systems that complement the world and environment by connecting with each other collaboratively in business, not in capitalism, such as Kate Raworth's TED Talk 'A Healthy Economy should be Designed to Thrive, not Grow'.[52]

As we each evolve personally, we are also advancing globally, expanding in universal awareness, shifting

50 B Marx Hubbard and C Anderson, *52 Codes for Conscious Self Evolution: A process of metamorphosis to realize our full potential self* (Awakened Word, 2011)
51 Grace Chatting, 'Why *Not* to Return to Business as Usual after the Coronavirus' (2020), www.youtube.com/watch?v=PwS7jZx1TBs
52 K Raworth 'A Healthy Economy should be Designed to Thrive, not Grow' (TED Talk, 2018), www.youtube.com/watch?v=Rhcrbcg8HBw

into the new paradigm and emerging futures. Now is the time to get things right, to be a part of bringing healing to the world. And with this, you and I become evolutionary people, enjoying a healthy and different relationship with our loved ones in spirit. No longer trapped in the grip of grief, we make a valuable contribution to all the brighter tomorrows. In nourishing our soul, we become resilient and whole so the world around us becomes more whole.

Suggestions to help you

- Embrace the fact that evolution is an experience of constantly growing and changing.

- Become as fascinated as I am by the scientific evidence in favour of spirituality.

- Follow the evolving discussions I have referenced in this chapter.

- Be open to a change of perspective on all levels of consciousness and spirituality as the evolving individual you are.

- Take comfort from the evidence to suggest what happens to our loved ones in the life between lives.

- Rejoice in the realisation that the reality we experience in the material world is definitely not the only one that exists.

- Learn from the experiences I have shared of my own spiritual evolution.

- Consider enlisting the help of a good evidential medium to help you connect with your loved one. It may well help you immensely on your own spiritual evolution.

- Investigate the amazing SoulPhone project. This is really happening in our lifetime!

- Decide to evolve to live as the multi-dimensional being you truly are.

Consider this: if the emotion of grief with its lowest of vibrational frequencies has brought about any trans-formational changes for you, just imagine what living more consistently from a place of joy will do.

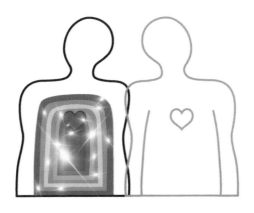

Conclusion

I have shown throughout this book that knowledge and understanding give you back a sense of power over what feels like a disempowering experience: the death of a loved one. I have guided you through the journey of self-discovery and advancement by providing tools and suggestions to help you help yourself, and others, for many years to come. I hope that you will be kind and compassionate with yourself as the transition in your own personal grief journey may take you weeks, months or even years.

Change perspectives as you desire and choose to. Shift your consciousness, successfully evolve through the transition to become strong and resilient, taking the opportunity for spiritual growth and expansion by attending to the continuing journey of your soul to become the very best version of yourself. This will impact every aspect of your life – your relationships, work and business – positively and personally.

Through my own therapeutic knowledge, experiences, studies and discoveries during my personal grief journey, along with case studies and scientific evidence, I have taken you above and beyond previous conscious understandings to a deeper awareness of yourself as a physical, emotional, spiritual and energy being. A multi-dimensional being. I've encouraged you to shift from living an ordinary life to an extraordinary life, reconnecting to the newfound riches and insights of an evolutionary person.

It is with the most delightful sense of joy that I have been able to introduce you to the awareness and understanding that you can still be in communication with your loved one. That your love for each other never dies; it continues outside of space and time. Your relationship with your loved one can continue and be constant, creating a new and fulfilling place in your heart which will provide a deep sense of peace, love and emotional security, *filling the hole of your loss with a wonderful glowing, vibrant energy of strength, substance, joy and excitement.*

Knowing this is possible will reduce your fears, worries, anxieties and stress. In reality, how often did you call your mum, dad, nan, grandad, partner, friend, child when they were still here in this life? Sometimes, it's not as often as you may think because you knew they were there, and so it is with spirit. In time, you may not feel the need to think of your loved one constantly because you will know they are truly always there for you. Love never dies. You can get on with life in the here and now, secure in the knowledge your loved one has a new life to get on with in spirit. This brings much calm and happiness.

How would it impact on the world if everyone developed their natural abilities to talk to their loved ones in spirit? It would bring compassion and peace as everyone would be coming from a place of mutual love and respect in heartfelt service to others, the environment, the creatures and wildlife, political and social structures. There would indeed be peace on earth for us all.

I would really appreciate your thoughts on this, or anything we've discussed in the book. You can find my contact details on 'The Author' page at the end.

Bibliography

Bonanno, GA *The Other Side of Sadness: What the new science of bereavement tells us about life after loss* (Basic Books, 2010)

Dispenza, J *Becoming Supernatural: How common people are doing the uncommon* (Hay House 2017)

Dispenza, J *You Are the Placebo: Making your mind matter* (Hay House, 2014)

Eger, E *The Choice: A true story of hope* (Rider, 2018)

Hawkins, D *Power vs Force: An anatomy of consciousness* (Veritas, 2012)

Helmstetter, S *The Power of Neuroplasticity: The breakthrough scientific discovery that every thought you think rewires your brain and changes your life* (CreateSpace, 2014)

Jeffers, S *Feel the Fear and Do it Anyway: How to turn your fear and indecision into confidence and action* (Vermillion, 2007)

Kahn, M *Everything is Here to Help You: A loving guide to your soul's evolution* (Hay House, 2018)

Kessler, D *Finding Meaning: The sixth stage of grief* (Rider, 2019)

Kübler-Ross, E *On Death and Dying* (Macmillan, 1969)

Lipton, BH *The Biology of Belief: Unleashing the power of consciousness, matter and miracles* (Hay House, 2015)

Lupo, LJ *Remember, Every Breath is Precious: Dying taught me how to live* (White Crow Books, 2018)

Marx Hubbard, B; Anderson, C *52 Codes for Conscious Self Evolution: A process of metamorphosis to realize our full potential self* (Awakened Word, 2011)

Moore, T *Dark Nights of the Soul: A guide to finding your way through life's ordeals* (Penguin Random House, 2004)

Newton, M *Destiny of Souls: New case studies of life between lives* (Llewellyn, 2001)

Newton, M *Journey of Souls: Case studies of life between lives* (Llewellyn, 2004)

Newton, M *Life Between Lives: Hypnotherapy for spiritual regression* (Llewellyn, 2004)

Newton, M *Memories of the Afterlife: Life between lives stories of personal transformation* (Llewellyn, 2009)

Pitstick, MR; Schwartz, GE *Greater Reality Living: Integrating the evidence for eternal consciousness into your daily life* (CreateSpace, 2018)

Polkinghorne, JC *One World: The interaction of science and theology* (Templeton Foundation Press, 2007)

Weiss, B *Many Lives, Many Masters: The true story of a prominent psychiatrist, his young patient and the past-life therapy that changed both their lives* (Piatkus, 1994)

Weiss, B *Same Soul, Many Bodies* (Piatkus, 2004)

Acknowledgements

It is due to the incredible love and dedication of my amazing husband and partner John, a man in a million whose constant patience, kindness and calm never ceases to amaze me and without such this book would not have come into existence. His endless encouragement and belief that this book needed to be written kept me going during times of wobbles and doubts. For allowing me to use him as a sounding board, for knowing me and understanding me like no other and for helping me to clarify what I wanted to say at times using his own bereavement and palliative care counselling experience. For being such an intelligent, gifted, conscious, spiritual human being, for being my great companion and soul mate, thank you for choosing me as yours and journeying this life learning experience together.

To my dear friend and earth angel, Tracy White, who was my eyes, ears, arms and heart when I could not physically be there for Jack. Whose love, kindness, loyalty and compassion went far beyond friendship in many ways that only she, Jack and I know. I am eternally grateful.

To all of my fantastically loyal friends and family who over a lifetime of years put up with me forever being busy working, focused on some sort of project or another like this book. Especially our beautiful daughters, inside and out, Jeneen and Laura who I am immensely proud of for their own individual achievements along with their respective partners Stewart and Adam. Amazing grandson Josh with his very lovely partner Nuala, their delightful daughter Lyla and his brothers Ben and Kai. With an extra special thank you to my brother John and partner Pip for running marathons and parachuting, 'jumping for Jack' in honour of his memory during the Normandy Landing memorials following Jack leaving this earthly place.

With much gratitude and thanks to all the people who have supported or contributed to this book with such a generosity of spirit. In particular, my counselling supervisor Dr Rosa Hubbard Ford, dear friend and mentor Grace Chatting, reiki teacher and spiritual adviser Jennie McDowell and Nichola Chant for her enthusiasm and always championing me.

For the very much appreciated invaluable input of Lucy Matthews, Louise Turton, Cathy Regan and Alyss Thomas of Western Women Mean Business Membership Group and the kindred support of that group. Thank you for talking with me Sue, Claire, Julie and Tina.

To Liz Gordon for her additional insights.

To all the wonderful people who permitted me to share their personal grief and therapeutic stories and experiences in this book in the hope it will help others.

I would like to thank the many clients I've had the privilege of spending time working therapeutically with and from whom I have learnt and continue to learn so much; a massive thank you for putting your trust and vulnerable selves in my hands. A deep and heartfelt thank you to each and every one of you.

To my many inspiring teachers and students over the years; all have given me so much knowledge and pleasure in this infinite cycle of teaching and learning.

All my dear friends near and far, especially Sue, Janine and Myron, Alan and Lindsey, Cathy and Dave, Rose, Kim, Patricia, Andrea, D, Sue, Mina, Sarah and Debs.

With a special recognition to 'Team Plymouth': Mark, Lou, Carol, Bev, Hazel, Tracy and Naomi for your dedication and support for so many years.

For the marvellous coaching and guidance of Lucy McCarraher for making this book writing opportunity possible and everyone involved in producing it at Rethink Press.

To my mother, father and grandmothers, my sisters and brothers, Wendy, Paul, Linda, Mark and John, and to everyone in my family and beyond I have either learnt from or through in this incredible school of life.

And, most especially, my brilliantly multi-dimensional son Jack. From whom I have learnt so much that has enhanced my life and work and is now in spirit, without whom this book would not have even been conceived and who has helped me to write it in ways I could never have imagined.

With love,
Joy xxx

The Author

Joy Sackett Wood, BA (hons), PGCE, MNCS (Senior Accredited), MHS (Accredited), MUKRF

Instinctively entrepreneurial by nature and with a very varied and diverse professional background, Joy has worked among many occupations and businesses spending time in the fashion industry as a designer, has a degree in philosophy and theology and a PGCE in Religious Education. She taught in the education sector for over twenty-five years, before transferring her skills into her present successful counselling, coaching and ever evolving therapeutic work.

Established in her private practice since 2008, she has a rich amount of both personal and professional experience. Joy's journey as a woman in constant evolution of herself and her soul has taken her from a humble background to a happy and fulfilled life which was traumatically disrupted on 27 October 2018 by the death of her son.

This book is a testimony to Joy's strength of spirit, integrity and resilience as she supports you through what may be the most painfully challenging time of your personal and working life, offering you insights, encouragement, tools and suggestions to help you through the pain of your grief, enabling you to progress through the trauma to transforming your life.

🌐 www.joysackettwood.com

f www.facebook.com/Joysackettwood/

in www.linkedin.com/joy-sackett-wood-79176538/

🐦 https://twitter.com/joysackettwood

📷 www.instagram/joysackettwood/

Printed in Great Britain
by Amazon

55792077R00135